D0538999

WE COULD'VE FINISHED LAST WITHOUT YOU

WE COULD'VE
FINISHED LAST
WITHOUT YOU

An Irreverent Look At The Atlanta Braves,
The Losingest Team In Baseball For The Past 25 Years

BOB HOPE

LONGSTREET PRESS
Atlanta, Georgia

Published by
LONGSTREET PRESS, INC.
2150 Newmarket Parkway
Suite 102
Marietta, Georgia 30067

© Copyright 1991 by Bob Hope

All rights reserved. No part of this book may be reproduced in any
form or by any means without the prior written permission of the
Publisher, excepting brief quotes used in connection with reviews,
written specifically for inclusion in a magazine or newspaper.

Printed in the United States of America

1st printing, 1991

Library of Congress Catalog Number 90-063895

ISBN 0-929264-84-3

This book was printed by R. R. Donnelley & Sons,
Harrisonburg, Virginia. The text was set in ITC Zaph Book Light
by Typo-Repro Service, Inc., Atlanta, Georgia.
Jacket Design by Laura Ellis.
Book design by Jill Dible.

Photographs by Walter Victor

To my father, Eugene W. Hope,
and my father-in-law, A. D. Snow

TABLE OF CONTENTS

INTRODUCTION

If failure in baseball were fatal, the Atlanta Braves would have died a long time ago. Since moving to Atlanta from Milwaukee in 1966, the Braves have had the worst record in the major leagues.

They suffered through the pain of last place finishes eight times, a record of futility matched only by the San Diego Padres in their early years as an expansion team. However, the Braves have lost more games overall than the Padres or any other team. San Diego is the only team that had a worse record in the decade of the 1970s; another expansion team, the Seattle Mariners, was the only team with a worse record in the 1980s. But no other team comes close to the Braves' total of 2,137 losses out of 3,975 games over the past twenty-five years.

In fact, no team in American sports history has put together a longer span of ineptitude. The Chicago Cubs went a half century without a pennant, but the Cubbies were occasionally involved in pennant races and had winning teams as often as not. The old Philadelphia A's lost a lot, but they also won a lot, even dethroning the mighty Yankees of the late 1920s. The Washington Senators are remembered as losers, but they had their seasons in the sun. They were American League champions three times and even won the World Series in 1924. The old saying about Washington, "First in war, first in peace, and last in the American League," was somewhat exaggerated. The musical *Damn Yankees* made the Senators more glamorous and notorious as losers than they actually were.

The same thing happened to the Cleveland Indians. The modern Indians are viewed by the sports community as baseball's big losers. The movie *Major League* even used the Indians as its model of the ultimate in dismal baseball failure. But the Indians aren't even in the same league as losers with the Braves. Cleveland had only five cellar-dwelling experiences over the past quarter-century, compared to the Braves' eight. Furthermore, over the past five seasons the Braves have had a .402 winning percentage, forty-two points lower than the next-worst Indians. Those kinds of numbers will get you the red-carpet treatment in Las Vegas. Last place has become the home of the Braves.

The old St. Louis Browns were a disaster on the field before they moved to Baltimore to become the Orioles. Team owner Bill Veeck joked that once when a fan called to ask what time the game started, he responded, "What time can you be here?" The Browns would wait. But only twice did the Browns ever finish last.

Other sports don't offer legitimate contenders for the top futility spot. The Los Angeles Clippers in basketball have had a solid streak of frustrations, and possibly the new NBA expansion teams can eventually achieve traditions of failure, but it will take years.

NFL teams are safe because the season's too short to establish first-rate losers. Between the league's efforts to maintain parity and a playing season of only sixteen games, it's almost impossible for any one team to be miserable year after year after year.

The point of all this is not to be critical of the Braves. The team is like an old "Peanuts" comic strip where Charlie Brown asks himself, "How can we lose when we're so sincere?" The Braves, like Charlie and his gang, have been sincere enough and have always tried their best. They just haven't been as good as the teams they play against.

I know they tried hard. I was there watching and cheering and crying. I started working for the team part-time as an usher when I was seventeen years old and it was in its first Atlanta season, and I continued to work for them for the next fifteen years, eventually becoming vice president of the team. Now I'm on the Braves' board of directors.

Believe me, we tried everything we could think of to win.

I'm absolutely certain we're about to break out of our rut. I think. We've just finished a stretch of four last-place seasons in five years, but we're losing with better players. In fact, it looks like we have a lot of good young players. Dave Justice was National League Rookie of the Year last season. Ron Gant was Comeback Player of the Year, although I'm not quite certain where he came back from or that he was ever that good in the first place. But now he looks great. Players like Justice and Gant look amazingly unlike past Braves who seemed out of place in big-league uniforms.

Talented young players, we've noticed, develop into good older players. They are the ones who win. We've tried to build at times in the past with young players. Sadly, we just proved that bad young players grow up to be bad old players. The Braves never got any better. We'd put together a lineup of youngsters and plan to let them improve over the years. We'd call it a five-year plan, but five years later we were just as bad as ever. The only movement in our youth movements was downhill.

Our most recent five-year plan culminated with a season that began with only two wins in the first fifteen games and didn't get much better. Dale Murphy, who had been "Mr. Brave" for twelve seasons, was traded to the Phillies. Bobby Cox, the general manager of the team, was ordered down from the front office to become field manager for his second term. He finished the same place he did his first term. Last. Nick Esasky, a much-ballyhooed free agent signed after hitting thirty home runs the year before with the Red Sox, played only nine games as a Brave and was out for the remainder of the year with something called "persistent vertigo." Our pitching staff, considered before the season our greatest strength, finished the year with a 4.57 earned run average, easily the worst in the big leagues.

Things will get better. We're always intent on winning. In fact, most of the time, we think we're right on the verge of winning big. Today I write that we're near the end of our losing era. I would have written the same thing any spring during the last twenty-five years. This time, though, I think I'm right. But, then, I thought I was right in the past, too.

1

THE START OF THE BRAVES' NEW WORLD

When the Braves arrived in Atlanta for the 1966 season, it was a time to celebrate. The South was welcoming its first big-league sports franchise of any kind. The Braves were moving into a brand-new stadium, built in just fifty-one weeks especially to lure the team from Milwaukee, where it was fighting a losing battle for survival.

The announcement of the Braves' move South was a dream come true. Baseball wasn't totally new to Atlanta. We had the Atlanta Crackers, who were called the "Yankees of the South" in those minor-league years of playing teams like the Nashville Vols, Chattanooga Lookouts, Little Rock Travelers, Birmingham Barons, and New Orleans Pelicans. The Crackers built a wonderful tradition of winning at rickety old Ponce de Leon Park. A home-run-hitting outfielder for the team, Bob Montag, was every bit as popular in Atlanta as Mickey Mantle was in New York.

The only contact Atlanta had with the big leagues consisted of newspaper articles about Crackers who made it there. Tim McCarver was a popular catcher in Atlanta who made it to St. Louis. Mike Shannon and Johnny Lewis also made it to the bigs. The most popular Atlanta youngster was an eighteen-year-old named Eddie Mathews, who beat his chest black and blue learning to play third base for the Crackers and then made it to the Hall of Fame with the Braves in Milwaukee.

The glory years of the Crackers had faded by the mid 1960s, and the arrival of a major-league baseball team seemed to most Atlantans as probable as the landing of a troop from Mars. When it happened, it was exciting, important, and almost mystical, something that big cities had and we could only dream about.

The mayor of Atlanta at that time, Ivan Allen, Jr., believed in the city like no one else, and that belief showed in the progress it was making. He was mayor when glass towers started replacing stumpy red-brick buildings, and a hotel with a revolving restaurant on top replaced the old Heart of Atlanta Motel with its high diving board as the most exotic place in town. For years modern freeways had been under construction, converging on Atlanta from north, south, east, and west. But when drivers reached Atlanta, they would have to exit and navigate the city streets. In 1965, though, the work was done and all the freeways interconnected. Atlanta was taking on the look of a big city. It sounds fairly mundane now, but it was very big stuff back then.

Mayor Allen had worked for what seemed like years to get a baseball team, despite the problem of not having a place to play. Ponce de Leon Park had served its purpose for the Crackers but was not a big-league facility. It looked like virtually every other run-down minor-league park. It was special, we thought, because a magnolia tree grew on a hill in front of the outfield fence. Where else could a fielder run into a tree while attempting to catch a fly ball? It also had railroad tracks on top of the bank in right field, where freight trains would pass noisily during the games. Legend noted that Bob Montag's longest home run was hit 150 miles, landing in a freight car and ending up in Chattanooga.

By the time the city started thinking seriously about big-league sports, Ponce de Leon's best days were over. The Crackers weren't drawing the large crowds of the past, and the only other activities there were a few high school football games and an occasional special event. The biggest crowd in its history was 23,000 for a Yankees exhibition game featuring Babe Ruth. The second-biggest was for a contest between two Indian tribes. A local promoter named Jay Lee Friedman packed the place for an Indian "capture the stick" contest. Two tribes entered the field in full war dress, and after a quick flurry of dust and motion, the action stopped. The stick had been captured. The game was over. Jay Lee had to refund the ticket money. Such was the state of sports in Atlanta when the Braves arrived.

Mayor Allen went after and got big-league sports. He had wined and dined Charlie Finley, owner of the Kansas City A's, nearly convincing him to move the A's south. Finley chose Oakland instead. Then, as if by magic, the word came that the Braves were moving to Atlanta and a brand-new, modern stadium was being built, one that could also accommodate professional football someday.

Life suddenly became different for Atlanta and the South. The city instantly became the unchallenged heart of the Southeast, a thriving metropolitan area about to jump over the remarkable one-million population mark. The Braves would become the only major-league team in the Southeast, drawing its fans from Georgia, Tennessee, the Carolinas, Alabama, and Florida. Atlanta would be listed every day in the major-league standings in newspapers across the nation, along with New York, Chicago, Los Angeles, Philadelphia, and other such worldly places. Attendance would surely be no problem, and it was opening up radio and TV possibilities for baseball in a whole new part of the country. The team couldn't fail.

Atlanta was totally different from Milwaukee. The Braves had some early success in Wisconsin after moving from Boston following the 1952 season. The Milwaukee Braves finished second, third, second, second again, and then in 1957 they won the National League pennant and beat the Yankees in the World Series. The first issue of a new magazine named *Sports Illustrated* had Eddie Mathews on the cover celebrating the championship. Attendance soared to more than two million.

Eventually, reality set in. The Braves of the early 1960s weren't in the race each year. Milwaukee was never a huge city in the first place, and it was just a short distance from Chicago, home of both the Cubs and White Sox. Then in 1961 the Washington Senators moved to Minnesota, became the Twins, and further diminished the Braves' territory. It became obvious to all baseball experts that Milwaukee was no longer a practical location for a team. Thus, the move to Atlanta was a logical decision.

The start in the South was auspicious. On April 12, 1966, a crowd of 50,671 saw the South's first regular-season major-league baseball game. Mayor Allen triumphantly threw out the first ball. By season's end, the first Atlanta team tripled Milwaukee's previous season's attendance, despite a fifth-place finish by the Braves.

Admittedly, the Braves' success at the gate owed much to the newness of the big-league game in Atlanta. "There was a novelty about the whole thing," the team's catcher Joe Torre recalled. "At a game against the Giants, there were 45,000 fans in the stands, and you could hear a pin drop. The fans didn't know what to do at a ball game."

Over the next few years, it seemed the Braves were on the right track. In 1967, they remained in the pennant race until September. During the season, a little-used, twenty-seven-year-old relief pitcher was given a try as a starter. Phil Niekro went on to become a fixture for the Braves. He won three hundred games in his twenty-four big-league seasons and finished as the oldest starting pitcher in the history of the game.

Then in 1969, it happened: the Braves won the National League's Western Division title. Yankee World Series veteran Clete Boyer played third base on the team; Cardinal World Series veteran Orlando Cepeda played first. Niekro won twenty games, and the great Hank Aaron matched his uniform number with forty-four home runs. Rico Carty, the "beeg boy" from the Dominican Republic who wouldn't deign to take the bat from his shoulder until he had two strikes against him, hit .342.

But in 1970 the Braves inexplicably fell back to mediocrity, and the losing continued for the next three seasons. Little noticed in the events of the '71 season was Aaron's 600th home run. Only 16,000 fans showed up the afternoon he hit it, but it was a major milestone: the unofficial beginning of his chase of Babe Ruth's home run record.

In 1973, Aaron, Dave Johnson, and Darrell Evans became the first three teammates ever to hit forty or more home runs in a season, but the feat made few headlines as Aaron continued his pursuit of Ruth's record. Hundreds of news reporters followed the Braves' every game — not just sportswriters but people like Tom Brokaw and Edwin Newman, known for covering world affairs rather than the baseball beat.

Then on April 8, 1974, at 9:07 p.m., 53,775 fans saw Aaron hit the record-breaking homer in Atlanta. The full stadium stood cheering for nearly ten minutes as Hank rounded the bases and was met at home plate by his entire team, as well as a swarm of photographers. It was the year of the streaking craze, and the most unnoticed streaker of the year was the woman who chose to disrobe in the leftfield bleachers while Aaron circled the diamond.

The 1974 season had other highlights. Buzz Capra led the league's starting pitchers with a 2.28 ERA. Reliever Tom House led all pitchers in the league with a 1.92 ERA. Ralph Garr topped the league in hitting at .353. Niekro once again won twenty. The team finished in a respectable second place. Maybe, we thought, the Braves were on their way to winning again.

Not so. The team barely escaped last place the next season. They were losing and losing bad. Since the other two teams in the city of Atlanta, the Falcons of the NFL and the Hawks of the NBA, were losing too, the Atlanta newspapers dubbed the city "Losersville USA."

Then, in 1976, TV mogul Ted Turner bought the team and promised success. He immediately signed big-league baseball's most notorious free agent, Andy Messersmith, to a million-dollar contract. The former Dodger pitcher had challenged the legality of baseball's sacred reserve clause and won, opening the door for all future free agents to play out their contracts and switch teams. The Braves also obtained Darrel Chaney of the National League Champion Reds and Dodger home run champion Jim "the Toy Cannon" Wynn. Three other Dodgers—Lee Lacey, Tom Paciorek, and Jerry Royster—were also acquired in the trade that sent Dusty Baker to the Dodgers. Wynn and Lacey were class veterans and Paciorek and Royster "sure bet" youngsters. Garr was sent to the White Sox for All-Star outfielder Ken Henderson. In June, first baseman Willie Montanez was obtained from the Giants, and he finished the year hitting .321.

On paper, the Braves couldn't lose. On the field, it was their first season in last place. And they continued in last place the next four seasons.

But the new decade revived the dormant club. The 1980 team jumped over .500 with an 81-80 record. Then, after drifting back into the second division in 1981, the Braves—led by young outfielder Dale Murphy—won the National League West in 1982. They almost won in 1983 too. Murphy was named the league's Most Valuable Player both seasons.

After 1983, however, the Braves started sinking again, and they're still sunk.

Even after I quit the Braves to see what life was like in the winning world, I still couldn't stay away from the team completely. I begged Ted Turner to put me on the board of directors, and he sent a note to all the other board members saying he'd elected me. That's how the Braves' board works.

So now I live in New York, watch the Braves every night of the summer on the SuperStation, and am influenced in my opinions about baseball by the New York media. When I attended the Braves board of directors meeting on opening day of 1988, I arrived in the big, posh boardroom of Turner Broadcasting with a folder full of spring-training stories and season predictions clipped from New York newspapers.

The team president and the general manager gave their assessments of the prospects for the upcoming 1988 season.

Granted, we finished ahead of only San Diego in our division and lost twenty-three more games than we won in 1987, but, they emphasized, we moved out of last place. We had turned the corner, they noted; we should be in the pennant race in 1988 and should certainly finish with more wins than losses.

Ted asked for reaction from the board members. Everyone nodded approval, except me.

"Hope, do you have something you want to say?" Ted asked. He knew I was concerned. I had written him a letter saying I'd about given up on our ability to field a good team, even volunteering to take over as chairman of the board, without pay, to try to straighten things out.

I squirmed at the thought of having to answer the question. I didn't want to seem unduly negative or cast a pall over a potentially great upcoming season. But I told them it just didn't look to me like the team was all that good. I also went ahead and read them the Braves "Outlook" for the upcoming season as printed in the New York *Daily News*: "Bleak. Pitiful. Beyond pain. Not enough hitting . . . and a legacy of losing that even a new manager would be powerless to change."

When I read the assessment, team president Stan Kasten responded by telling me the report was wrong. He guaranteed the Braves would finish the season above .500 and asserted that I had "become a jerk since moving to New York."

After a fast start, the Braves missed their goal of a winning season and finished last once again, this time losing five more games than any Braves team in history. I kept my thoughts to myself.

2

ALL THE RIGHT PLAYERS
AT THE WRONG TIMES

The bald assertion that a team had the worst record in sports during a quarter-century implies a degree of ineptitude that never really existed with the Braves. Position by position, they weren't that bad. In actuality, the Braves fielded one of the strongest lineups in the history of major-league baseball during those twenty-five years.

The outfielders included Hank Aaron, possibly the greatest player in the history of the game, World Series star Dusty Baker, and two-time league MVP Dale Murphy. The infield had all-stars Orlando Cepeda at first, Clete Boyer or Eddie Mathews at third, Rafael Ramirez or Zoillo Versalles at short, and Felix Millan at second. Batting champ Joe Torre was catcher. The pitching staff had Hall-of-Famer Gaylord Perry, future Hall-of-Famer Phil Niekro, and thirty-game winner Denny McLain, along with Pat Dobson, who was the leading pitcher in two World Series — neither with the Braves. The bullpen included the very best — Bruce Sutter, Hoyt Wilhelm, Al Hrabosky, and Cy Young Award-winner Steve Bedrosian.

They were all the right players. They just all played for Atlanta at the wrong times. Somehow team management could never put together all the pieces at any one time.

Over the twenty-five-year span of opening-day lineups, we had fourteen different starting first basemen, twelve second basemen, ten third basemen, twelve shortstops, fourteen catchers, fifteen leftfielders, fifteen centerfielders, and in right field, where Aaron was the mainstay for years, only nine different starters. In all, 345 different players appeared in Braves uniforms during that time, a league record.

The roster also included some of the most unusual players in baseball history. Hank and Tommie Aaron set the all-time record for career home runs by brothers at 768. Hank hit 755 and Tommie thirteen. Phil and Joe Niekro both pitched for the Braves and finished their careers with the most victories in history by brothers at 538. Phil won 318 and Joe 220.

An Atlanta-Fulton County Stadium usher, Rob Belloir, quit and returned a decade later to play shortstop for the Braves. Another shortstop, Leo Foster, set a league record by hitting into a triple play and two double plays in his first big-league game.

An assortment of players had their last hoorahs as Braves, including former thirty-game winner McLain, who had a three-game-winning season in Atlanta; Joe Pepitone, who was obtained one day and sold the next after refusing to play because he lost his toupee; Satchel Paige, who earned his pension as a Brave but never appeared in a game; *Ball Four* author Jim Bouton, who pitched his way through the Braves minor-league system for one last big-league start in Atlanta; and Terry Forster, a fat relief pitcher made famous by David Letterman's description of him as a "tub of goo."

On the other hand, we also had players who probably never should have been in the big leagues. Left-handed pinch-hitter Glenn Clark went to bat four times before it was known he was blind in his right eye—the one closest to the pitcher. Bob Didier, a slow, mediocre-fielding and light-hitting catcher, jumped from Class-A Greenwood, South Carolina, to the big leagues to become the nineteen-year-old starter for the 1969 division-winning Braves and then vanished from the big leagues forever. Bob Uecker readily admitted he was a lousy player but was able to corral Phil Niekro's knuckleball by "chasing it until it stopped rolling."

Pitcher Pascual Perez was already famous when he signed as the highest-paid journeyman pitcher ever for the New York Yankees. He initially earned his renown—along with his nickname "I-285"—with the Braves when he got lost driving to the stadium on Atlanta's perimeter highway, circled the city for hours, and missed the game.

An assortment of sure-fire future superstars bucked destiny with the Braves. A team often ranks good-looking young prospects based on great players of the past. The Braves had a long line of "looks like a young" Hank Aarons or Eddie Mathewses, or even Warren Spahns or Lou Burdettes from the team's Milwaukee heritage.

Curtis Moore, Gene Holbert, Taylor Duncan, Don Young, Ken Smith, and Brad Komminsk all could swing the bat "like a young Aaron." Regrettably, none was ever able to swing it anywhere close to the older Aaron as they got older.

Jamie Easterly, Mike McQueen, Derek Lilliquist, and George Stone—each was the "best left-handed pitcher since Warren Spahn," which said more about the lack of Braves left-handed pitching than it did about their big-league potential.

Occasionally a player's potential would transcend modest Braves comparisons. Outfielder Barry Bonnell looked "just like a young Joe DiMaggio" after he hit .300 his first season with the Braves. No comparisons were made the next year when he hit .240 or the year after that when he was traded to Toronto. Al Santorini was the "next Bob Feller." He lost his only Braves start and lasted only three innings.

Some players' performances belied their names. Shortstop Pat Rockett wasn't. Neither was Hank Small small. Outfielder Jim Wynn didn't, at least while he was a Brave. But pitcher Bob Walk did . . . so often that he was traded to the Pirates, where he didn't. And pitcher Adrian Devine was only average.

There's a saying in sports that players learn more from losing than from winning. Thus, many of the best managers and coaches were frequently ordinary players on losing teams. The Braves' history supports the theory. In 1990, the American League Champion Oakland A's were managed by former

Braves third baseman Tony LaRussa, who had also led the team to the World Championship the previous year. In the 1989 play-offs, his A's beat the Toronto Blue Jays, managed by former Brave Cito Gaston. The Mets won the World Series in 1986 and their division in 1988 with former Braves second baseman Davey Johnson as manager.

In all, two dozen former Braves are coaches or managers in the big leagues. The most famous hitting instructor in the game today is former Brave Walt Hriniak; he learned his techniques from his predecessor, former Brave Charlie Lau.

The most innovative pitching coach in the big leagues is thought to be Tom House of the Texas Rangers. He's known for such unique coaching techniques as having pitchers warm up their arms by throwing footballs instead of baseballs. House, too, was a Braves player, the ace of the relief staff in the early- to mid-1970s.

House, by the way, was also innovative during his playing days. He has a doctorate from the University of Southern California, and while he was studying for his masters, his wife Karen attended class in his place during baseball season. Also, when I prepared a report on how the other major-league baseball teams marketed themselves, House used that as the basis for his master's thesis. Karen and I should at least have honorary degrees for our work.

3

THE ART OF LOSING

The Braves were sinking further into last place in the late summer of 1990 and had just finished a particularly dismal stretch. Phil Niekro, retired as a pitcher and returned to the team as bullpen coach, was changing out of his uniform when a pitcher looked at him in frustration.

"This team's just not as bad as we're playing. We shouldn't be in last place," the pitcher said.

"Maybe we are and maybe we should," was Niekro's simple response. He had heard the whine of frustration before.

Being a loser is like being mugged—one of those things that happen to others, not to you. Players seldom come to the realization that they are contributors to a losing cause. "Bad" teams are comprised of twenty-five "good" players, mostly looking for a way out. The losing is generally credited to the "team," an amorphous gathering, all of whom are blameless.

When Dave Johnson played second base for the Braves, he couldn't make all the defensive plays a big-league second baseman is supposed to make. He'd regularly bungle routine grounders, then lash out at the condition of the field. "The ball hit a rock and took a bad bounce," he once reported to a sportswriter, effectively rapping the groundskeepers for not doing their job.

"The only rock in the infield is on Dave Johnson's shoulders,'' a veteran of the Atlanta ground crew wryly responded.

A player on a losing big-league team lives through frustrations and often causes them. Al Jackson was a sturdy little left-hander for the original New York Mets, a club that finished last each of its first four seasons. Jackson hurled fifteen innings of three-hit ball once, only to lose on two errors by teammate "Marvelous Marv" Throneberry. Marv was legendary for his capacity to contribute to losing causes. In his uniform, he resembled Mickey Mantle . . . until he picked up a baseball or bat. If he ever hit the ball, he could hit it out of sight. He just didn't hit it very often. His fielding was even worse. Once, in a magnificent minor-league effort, he dropped an easy fly ball for an error, picked up the ball and flung it backwards as he wound up to throw, and finally threw it wild in an effort to get the runner out at third. The hitter, who should have been out, scored on three Marv Throneberry errors on the same play. Marv must have been a star someplace to earn his way to the big leagues, but he epitomized losing once he got there.

The old, lovable Mets were notorious losers. The same Casey Stengel who led the Yankees to ten World Series led the Mets to the worst won-loss record of any team in the twentieth century. And as much as fans say they loved those adorable, losing Mets in hindsight, the fact that they didn't draw a million fans their first season suggests that the losing wasn't all that much fun when it was actually happening.

The famous Stengel question of those early years rings out loud and clear for any losing team: "Can't anybody here play this game?"

If players hate to accept responsibility for losing, management hates it even more. Losing is clearly, in management's minds, the fault of the players who "haven't delivered on their potential." The blame doesn't fall on the bad players, mind you, but on the most visible people on the team, the stars.

At his induction into the Hall of Fame in 1990, Joe Morgan said that being traded from the losing Houston Astros to the winning Cincinnati Reds was critical to his achieving Hall of Fame status. In Houston, he was viewed as talented but hampered by a bad attitude, as if it were imperative to remain cheerful in defeat. In Cincinnati, he was a team leader and Most Valuable Player on two world championship teams. On either team he would have been a star, but results of his stardom would have been far different if he had stayed with Houston.

The Braves' biggest stars suffered similarly. The rap dropped by management on Hank Aaron was, "All he can do is hit home runs." The fact that he broke virtually every hitting record in the book and led the league in fielding year in, year out, seemed to make little difference. He was finally traded to the Brewers because he wasn't worth what he was paid, according to management.

The record shows that the Braves never actually finished in last place until Aaron was traded. In fact, they finished second in his final season in Atlanta, fell to fifth the next year, and then reeled off a streak of four straight last places. He may have been the single thread holding them above the abyss of total failure.

Each season Niekro would win his twenty games, and someone in management would complain that he also had a high number of losses. Somehow management overlooked that the eight other players on the field with Phil weren't exactly the 1927 Yankees. Brett Butler was a "bad baserunner" on the Braves until he ended up with the Giants, who won the National League pennant. There his mistakes on the base-paths weren't noticed. His two hundred hits and runs scored each season were. Darrell Evans was "too old" for the Braves but went on to play thirteen more seasons after being traded, including a World Series and an All-Star Game.

However, whatever blame may be cast in the direction of the players, the purest form of pain is reserved for the managers. It is baseball tradition for management to say it can't fire the entire team so it fires the manager.

The same Whitey Herzog who was a dismal flop with the Texas Rangers and then fired by the Kansas City Royals became one of the best managers in baseball with the St.

Louis Cardinals. Yogi Berra was an instant winner everywhere he managed, only to be fired. Billy Martin won for three different teams as manager and was fired by all three. The Dave Johnson who led the Mets to the best record in baseball was fired when they faltered just one season.

When Ted Turner bought the Braves in 1976, he possessed the zealous commitment of all new team owners. He intended to make his mark, to make his team a big winner. Bill Bartholomay, who had already served as chairman of the Braves for a dozen years, said wryly about Ted, "He's about to find out about operating a business where you have no control over employee performance. You live and die each day with what the players do on the field. He's about to lose control of his fate."

After the initial losing season, Ted was undaunted. He told manager Dave Bristol he could manage the team for the "next hundred years" and signed him to a two-year contract. A month into the season, the Braves were in the midst of a record-setting seventeen-game losing streak, and during the All-Star break Ted held a meeting at which Bristol was voted out. It was decided to keep him through the remainder of the season and then let him go. In essence, Bristol lasted only the first three months of his hundred-year job.

He was one of more than a dozen Braves managers in Atlanta. One, Bobby Cox, was fired, returned to the team as general manager, fired his manager, and was forced to return to the dugout as manager again. Baseball managing is a strange and unforgiving life. Even Stengel was released by the Yankees after managing them to seven world championships. It makes little sense.

Branch Rickey, who gained immortality in baseball as the general manager of the Dodgers when he gave Jackie Robinson the chance to become the first black player in the majors, was a player, manager, and front-office executive during his career. Throughout baseball, Mr. Rickey was known for having all the players and all the money and never letting the two mix. He was a tightwad when it came to negotiating player contracts. He put together World Series winners for both St. Louis and Brooklyn, but the frustration of his life was his inability to build the Pittsburgh Pirates into a winner.

In baseball, legend repeated often enough becomes truth. One legend is that Mr. Rickey invented the batting helmet to protect Pittsburgh outfielder Ralph Kiner, not so much for when he was hitting as for when he was awkwardly playing the outfield. Supposedly, Kiner's first batting helmet had no air holes in it and formed a vacuum around his head during the first hot day-game. Holes had to be drilled in it to break the suction before they could pry it off his head.

Kiner, whatever his fielding flaws, was an amazing home-run slugger on a team that Mr. Rickey just couldn't breathe life into. After Kiner led the league in home runs in 1952 while the Pirates finished with a dismal record of 112 losses, Mr. Rickey sent him a contract for the next season with the maximum allowed pay cut of twenty-five percent. Kiner pleaded for a raise. "Son, where did the team finish last season?" Mr. Rickey asked him. "Last place," Kiner answered. "Son," observed Mr. Rickey, "I believe we could have finished last without you."

The Braves have had their share of multi-million-dollar players who have played well enough in last place to get raises. "Couldn't we have finished last without them, too?" we'd ask ourselves at the end of the season. But by the time the next spring arrived, we doled out the big money again in hopes of improvement.

The Braves keep changing players, keep changing managers, keep changing uniforms, waiting for the right combination to click. We've tried building with youth, having the lowest payroll and the youngest team in the league. We've also tried the free agent market, building the highest payroll in the league. Nothing has worked.

There's a saying about air travel that when you die and go to heaven you change planes in Atlanta. The World Series sounds like heaven but it must not be, because I'm not sure we can get there from Atlanta.

4

LOOKS LIKE A
FUN JOB TO ME

I grew up in Atlanta and had never been to a big-league base-ball game. For that matter, I'd never been to the North or even on an airplane. But I was a baseball fan. Back in seventh grade, after the Milwaukee Braves won the World Series, I had written Hank Aaron asking for an autograph. He never answered my letter, but he was still my favorite player — always. It seemed impossible he was coming to play in Atlanta. It was true, though; I was in my freshman year at Georgia State College, an urban school right in the middle of town, and just a half-dozen blocks away the new stadium was going up.

Going to class each day and then driving by to see how the stadium was coming along was my daily routine. Well, actually, there was considerably more to my daily routine. I was going to classes and working at the same time to earn the money for school. My job was on the graveyard shift at Mead Packaging Company, where I loaded giant rolls of craft paper on a machine that made them into corrugated cardboard for boxes. It was harder work than I wanted to do and great motivation to stay in college. I needed the money, so I kept right on working at what I considered a miserable job.

One day the idea-bulb went off in my head. If I had to work,

I ought to make a list of the ten jobs I'd like to have while working my way through school. Then I would apply for them. Maybe one would come through. The first place on my list was the Braves.

It's embarrassing to reveal how easy it was to get a job with the team. My father drove me to the stadium one morning and waited in the car while I went in to apply. There was no office to be found, but I ran into a man who turned out to be a former Braves minor-league catcher named Jim Hay. Jim took me to a trailer that served as his office and had me fill out an application to work as an usher at the home games. I told him I'd like a part-time job in the office if one became available, and he wrote a note on my application.

I took the ushering job and kept my regular job at Mead, and after I had ushered a few games, Jim asked me if I was still looking for a job in the office. I said yes, so he sent me to meet with Lee Walburn, the team's publicity director. Lee, a thin, easy-going former sportswriter with the *Atlanta Journal*, asked me if I knew how to keep baseball statistics. I realized that if I said no I'd be out of a job, so I lied. I was hired.

This was absolutely the greatest job in the history of the world for a kid going to college. I was the scoreboard operator during the games, and I updated the team's statistics sheets and wrote a page of "press notes" during the day. And I did anything else they wanted me to do. I loved it.

I'd go down to the dressing rooms before the games to get the starting lineups, so I got to know all the players. My hours were flexible. I'd take classes during the day, update the stats and write the press notes whenever I could find the time, and study while pushing ball and strike buttons on the scoreboard during the games.

Since I had been an usher, I could still do that for special events at the stadium. Once, while race riots were taking place in Atlanta, a James Brown concert was held at the stadium. They didn't want only black ushers, so I was the token white. Another time I was a "gofer" at a Barbra Steisand concert. Barbra refused to perform until someone found her a yellow rain slicker. I was assigned the task. I had no idea where to find one but had walked only about a hundred yards before I saw a policeman in the stadium tunnel wearing one. I was a hero, I thought. I also worked the 1966 Beatles concert at the stadium.

When I graduated, I had every intention of getting a serious job and leaving the Braves, but I was having too much fun. Lee made me his full-time assistant, a permanent part of the organization.

By this time I had moved away from my parents' home into one of the "Singles Only" apartment complexes that were sprouting everywhere. A local auto dealer provided me with a free car. A clothing manufacturer gave me free clothes. Restaurants would let me eat for nothing, just because I worked for a big-league team. I even got a lifetime supply of Lifebuoy soap, Gillette razors, and a variety of the other items sent to us in boxloads by the Braves' radio and TV sponsors. It was all because I worked for the Braves.

Baseball gives everyone associated with the team celebrity status in the community. I would make three or four speeches each week to civic clubs, schools, and business groups. Nothing special. Just sign autographs, give out bumper stickers and answer questions about the Braves. I'd serve on civic boards like United Way and the Boys Club with the heads of the biggest companies in town and would be called on as a celebrity emcee or contest judge for special events.

Once the International Shriners organization held its convention in Atlanta. More than fifty thousand fez-headed old men descended on the town for a week. I was invited to be a judge in the Shrine clown competition.

My instructions were to show up at the parking lot of the old Sears building at seven o'clock Sunday morning ready to select the best Shrine clown in the world. When I arrived, other judges joined me for the selection process, including Atlanta Flames hockey player Pat Quinn, who now coaches in the NHL. We were guided to a parking lot full of thousands of clowns and told to pick the best. When we asked what criteria to use, we were told to make up our own.

The process took hours. We'd line the clowns up in regiments and walk down the formation like generals inspecting an army. Occasionally we'd see a clown who struck our fancy and ask him to step to the front. We kept culling until we had a workable group of about a hundred. Then we pared it down to twenty.

As we were nearing completion of our project, the tension was growing. Not only were the clowns anxious to win; the wives of the clowns were intent on seeing their husbands honored as the best. Finally, when we had a group of six lined up for the final selection, one of the wives started verbally assaulting me. Her husband had been eliminated and she was mad. She demanded to know my qualifications for the job at hand.

"What right do you have to call yourself a judge?" she shouted. "What qualifies you to be the judge of a clown contest?"

Without a second's hesitation Pat Quinn came to my rescue: "Lady, this man is thoroughly qualified to judge clowns. He watches the Atlanta Braves play every day."

Another time, when I was a judge of the Georgia Junior Miss Contest, I cheated and didn't tell the other judges I was prejudiced; my wife had been a summer-camp counselor for the finalist from Athens. She was a senior at Clarke Central High School, and frankly, whether my wife was her counselor or not, I thought she was gorgeous. We ranked the girls one-to-ten in ten different categories. I gave her a ten in every category. The other judges on the panel assured me I was wrong to vote her so high, explaining that she was not a typical high school senior. I agreed with that observation. But even with my help, she finished runner-up to a cute, chubby-legged girl named Susie Whitted. I was stunned, but could only conclude that I was in error; Kim Basinger must not have been as great looking as I thought.

By the way, by finishing second in the Georgia contest, Kim qualified to enter the national Breck Shampoo competition that would select one girl to appear in Breck's upcoming magazine ad campaign. Kim won that contest, and it was the first big break of her show business career. I haven't seen her since the contest, and, sadly, she'll probably never know I'm the one to whom she owes all of her wealth and success.

Another perk of my job with the Braves was that I had a key to the stadium. If that doesn't sound like a big deal for a twenty-two-year-old, check this. One night at a party I saw a woman I really wanted to impress. Her date said his dream was to play on a big-league baseball field, so I gave him his chance. We went directly to the stadium, and at two o'clock in the morning, I turned on the lights and a group of us played a game. The stunt must have worked. I'm now married to that woman.

Occasionally, Lee would send me on the road with the team. That was no drudgery, either. We went to the best cities, stayed in the best hotels, worked at night, slept late, and had all day to do whatever we wanted. And, of course, hanging out with the players was a big thrill for me.

On my first trip I was nervous and self-conscious. I had never been on an airplane before, much less traveled with a major-league team. As soon as I got on the plane, I started overhearing the players talk about "going to Tiny's." They kept talking about the "action at Tiny's." "Can't wait to get to Tiny's." "Hope Tiny's is jumping tonight." No one talked to me about it, but I couldn't help overhear. By the time we arrived in Los Angeles, my imagination was reeling with visions of what kind of all-night club "Tiny's" must be.

When we got to the hotel, several of the players rushed to their rooms, saying they were changing clothes and would be right back down to the lobby to go to Tiny's. Another group of players didn't bother to change; they just paced anxiously around the lobby. Finally they thought to ask me if I'd like to go along. I blurted yes and rushed to my room to change into a coat and tie.

They then marched me up the street to Tiny's, and promptly broke into laughter. I had fallen for one of their pranks. Tiny's was nothing but an all-night diner where they liked to go for coffee and ice cream.

Among the players, pranks seemed practically a vocation. A favorite was to replace a new rookie player's street shoes during the last game of a home stand with the ugliest, gaudiest shoes the trickster could find, giving the player no choice but to wear the shoes on the road trip.

On the bus trips between airport and stadium, a couple of players would always try to confuse the bus driver and get him lost. That was often not hard to do since most drivers were intimidated by the big-league club. "They can't beat us if they can't find us," one of the players once commented when a bus driver was lost during a losing streak. Someone would always yell, "Let's go, bussy," when it was time to pull out, as if the yell were a baseball tradition.

The hotels back then weren't all spectacular. We stayed at the old Roosevelt in New York until the night there was a shooting in the hall outside one of our rooms. And in San Diego, before a modern hotel row was constructed, we stayed at an old Hilton downtown. The players always joked that the only other people there were over seventy. Once, as if to prove the point, the national "Cootiette" convention was being held there. "Cooties" were World War I veterans, and these were their wives. There were hundreds of them.

The Cootiettes wore uniforms and marched in regiments up and down the halls of the hotel. The only ones under seventy were the Cootiette mascots, three women in their twenties. The players made a game of chasing the Cootiette mascots, but a sportswriter was the only one of us I ever saw catch one.

Yes, there were plenty of groupies on the road, but they weren't nearly as attractive as I had imagined. The players knew them all, and some showed up in several different cities. The relationship between them and the players was usually just casual, like with a bellhop or waitress at a hotel. The entire traveling group knew them, recognized them, and bantered with them, but there seemed to be little more to it.

Once in San Diego I went with a couple of players to get

breakfast at a Denny's restaurant up the street from the hotel. A couple of the groupies were already there and invited us to sit with them. After breakfast, one of the women held a cigarette up to her mouth and signaled for me to light it. I lit a match and she blew it out. I lit another one and she blew it out. "Stop blowing," I said. "I've never had a man tell me that," she smiled. I'd been had again.

A stripper named Morganna became the most notorious groupie. She gained her fame by rushing out on the field and kissing players, not just in baseball but in a variety of other sports. Her first conquest was Clete Boyer when he was about to go to bat at Atlanta-Fulton County Stadium during the 1969 pennant race. The photo of her kissing Boyer was selected the national Associated Press sports photo of the year. Some sport!

Back home, the office personnel worked hard for the team, and sometimes worked even harder to keep their minds off the team's poor performance on the field. But with our front-office staff, work was never dull.

Donald Davidson, the team's traveling secretary and my first real boss at the Braves, was the most remarkable of all our front-office personnel. Standing only four feet tall, he was one of the biggest characters in baseball. Donald had been with the club since it was in Boston, and there were more stories about him than any other official in the game. His fire-brand personality and prankster spirit put anyone of normal height at a disadvantage. Donald's antics created stories that turned into legend.

Although I joined the team as an usher, I soon became the scoreboard keeper on the new "million dollar" scoreboard at the stadium. I kept track of the runs, hits, errors, balls, strikes, and outs, and next to me in the booth overlooking the field was Red Mullins, the operator of the giant stadium message board, called the Fan-O-Gram. Donald was boss of the Fan-O-Gram Room, where we sat during the games.

Everyone called Donald the "director," and he played the part well. With a Girl Scout beanie on his head, dark glasses, and a long cigarette holder, he'd march about the booth barking orders to us during the games. He was always complaining about the Fan-O-Gram. The new Houston Astrodome had a scoreboard that displayed animation, and Donald was convinced the Fan-O-Gram should be able to do the same thing, if we only knew how to operate it right. The fact that it wasn't built for animation didn't inhibit his criticism.

Before one of the games, Red and I were working in the Fan-O-Gram room when two businessmen from General Indicator Corporation, maker of the message board, arrived to wait for Donald. They had never met him, so we knew they were in for a surprise. We listened as they anxiously discussed his complaints about their product. They waited a half-hour.

Abruptly the door to the room swung open and in pranced diminutive Donald in his director's outfit. Without noticing the two visitors, he started pacing the floor and shouting orders. "Red, take a Fan-O-Gram message," he ordered. "'Welcome.' No, make that 'A special Atlanta welcome.' No, make that 'A very special Atlanta welcome to Gerald Gentry and Peter Merritt of General Indicator Corporation of Pardeeville, Wisconsin, makers of the worst damn Fan-O-Gram in the National League.'"

Donald was particularly fun for the players, and often the brunt of their tricks. Once at a spring training game in Bradenton, Florida, a group of Braves players warned the stadium gatekeeper that a midget from the circus would try to crash the gate that day, pretending to be an official with the Braves.

"Don't let him in," they instructed.

The guard confronted Donald, and a fight broke out between the midget and the feeble, old security guard. The guard called the police to have Donald arrested before the players stepped in to save their little friend.

Then there was the time Donald went to war with a hotel manager in St. Louis and marched the entire team single file down the street to another hotel. And the time in New York when Donald couldn't push open the door of the men's room at the Roosevelt Hotel and was compelled to relieve himself in a potted plant in the lobby.

When Donald would get on the elevator with a group of players, he'd ask them to push the button for his floor. "Push it yourself," they'd respond, and the little man would have to wait for a stranger to reach the button and get him to his floor. The players loved the trick and Donald thrived on telling about it.

In bars Donald would buy drinks for everyone. But at his small size he couldn't hold much liquor himself. He once passed out drunk, toppled over into a suitcase, and the top slammed shut. The team searched half the night before finding him. He often started barroom brawls, but seldom was around to settle the score. That part was left up to the Braves players and other friends.

Once, for instance, professional baseball was holding its annual winter meetings in New Orleans. Donald was sitting with a group of Braves employees in the bar of the Marriott Hotel. The duo on stage asked the audience to be quiet so they could sing "Bojangles" a cappella, explaining that it was a special song to them and required complete silence. Donald has yet to hear the request. He did, however, hear the command from a man across the room to "shut up." Donald's reaction consisted of a series of four-letter words. Suddenly chairs were flying, and a shocked stranger found himself about to start a fistfight with a midget. "Stand up and fight," the man yelled, and Donald, just like in an old Vaudeville gag, snapped back, "I am standing up!"

During Donald's tenure, the Braves had two broadcasters who shared the announcing booth for radio and television games. Milo Hamilton was a polished Chicagoan whose resounding voice was matched by an astounding ego that seemed to clash all too often with players and front-office people. His sidekick was a former Braves relief pitcher, Ernie Johnson, who was every bit as down to earth as Milo was high and mighty. Most of the time the team's games were on radio only, but when a game was on both TV and radio, Donald would call the final inning on radio so Ernie could go down to the field for a post-game interview. The logistics worked fine, but Donald's voice was right out of the cartoons—the Elmer Fudd cartoons, to be exact. His announcing career ended when the Braves, according to Donald, "boo a one-wun wead in da ninth" and went into six extra innings with Donald on the mike. Listeners called in wondering what had happened to their radios.

Since Donald made all the team's travel arrangements, hotel managers always gave him the best suite in the house, and airlines always put him in first class—whether he paid for it or not. His tastes ran more to limousines than taxis. But Ted Turner had a rule that no employee could fly first class or stay in suites, much less travel in limousines. He thought it was frivolous. Donald never adhered to the rule and eventually paid the price.

Donald was the only employee Ted Turner ever fired. They just never got along. In some ways, they may have been too much alike. Donald was hired by the Houston Astros the day after his firing and spent the remainder of his career in the Houston front office.

It may only be a coincidence, but the serious losing for the Braves started the day Donald was fired. The team had a record of eight wins and four losses to start that 1976 season. Donald's wife, Patti, always claimed to be a witch, and her looks made the claim believable. She wasn't a midget, but she was small and had white skin set off against jet-black hair. When Ted fired Donald, Patti announced she had put a hex on the team. The Braves immediately lost thirteen games in a row, setting a National League record for longest losing streak.

The general manager of the Braves in that era was one of the more unusual and historic men in baseball. Bill Lucas was the first black man ever to run a big-league club. He was competent and easy-going and had a masterful way of dealing with everyone, including Ted Turner.

Bill had played in the Braves' farm system and later became the farm director, in charge of the entire minor-league system. Dale Murphy is the best example of the Braves minor-leaguers who developed and flourished under Bill. His youngsters formed the team that won the Braves' only division pennant in the 1980s.

He was only forty-one years old when he was named general manager of the team, making him the youngest general manager in the big leagues. Bill was one of baseball's truly special men.

Business manager Charles Sanders was another front-office personality. Charles was a tall, thin native of Hartwell, Georgia, who moved slowly, puffed on a pipe, and prided himself on being an accomplished Casanova. He was always my staunchest ally in the office, and, in return, I'd make sure he had the chance to escort the assortment of starlets who descended on games during publicity and promotional tours. When tennis star Jimmy Connors married a former "Playmate of the Year," Patti McGuire, there was some mock confusion in our office as to whether the forthcoming baby belonged to Jimmy or Charles. I had arranged for Charles to walk her to the pitcher's mound for her to throw out the first ball at a game.

Overall, we were a tightly knit troop operating the Braves' big-league baseball team the best way we knew how. We worked together every day at the stadium, had golf carts to get around the giant facility at lightning speed, and used walkie-talkies to keep in touch with each other. Granted, not everything worked perfectly all the time, like when the walkie- talkie frequency was the same as the public-address system and Donald blurted profanities to the entire crowd. But most of the time, when the gates of the stadium opened, we were ready for anything.

Occasionally, someone would try to break into our fraternity. Once, for instance, a mystery-man named John Alevisos was hired as general manager. None of us had ever heard of him, though he was a successful Boston businessman and had once worked as business manager of the Red Sox. But it was obvious that he had no respect for any of us, and he instantly became our enemy. We also heard rumors that he was approaching people from other ball clubs about taking our jobs.

He was a peculiar character. Plump, in his fifties, and constantly chewing sunflower seeds, he was Greek in heritage, and for no particular reason we were certain he had underworld connections. He also regularly voiced his suspicion that Ted Turner was crazy, noting that he himself was going to step in and take total control of the team to save it from Ted's incompetence. Ted's being crazy hardly seemed news to us, and crazy or not, he was the owner of the team. We were much more comfortable with Ted in charge in any state of mind than with the possibility of a coup by Alevizos.

John came to work at seven each morning and worked late into the night. He was energetic and intent on building the Braves into a winning organization . . . even if we weren't included in his plans. We also noticed he was a hypochondriac, regularly complaining about aches and pains. That was the only sign of weakness we needed. I gathered the troops in the front office to devise our plan. Each time any of us would see John, we'd ask him how he felt and advise him that he looked worn, tired, needed rest.

"John, are you okay?" I'd ask. "You don't look well. Go home. You're working too hard. Get some rest."

He started coming in later and later each day, leaving the office earlier and earlier each afternoon. Finally, after a couple of months, he was gone. We felt certain we had coaxed him to leave for health reasons, although Ted helped us by slamming the door on him at the end. We saved ourselves through our camaraderie.

Between pranks and being town celebrities, we had to take care of running the business affairs of the team. But frankly, it just never seemed much like work. Even while losing, times were good. And working for Lee Walburn was a delight. He had a nice way of encouraging you and telling you about qualities he saw in you that you wanted to believe were really there.

Lee believed in trying new things, in being an innovator. When the team decided to change the Braves' uniform design, we checked to find out why no baseball teams wore colored shirts then. It was because of tradition. In the old days only white and gray were used because colors would fade during the season. Since our new uniforms would be polyester, we went to a royal blue shirt. We thought it would be sensational. Hardly anyone noticed. The next season Charlie Finley's Oakland A's wore green shirts and got credit in all the national media as the first team with colored shirts. Didn't anyone even notice we were playing the previous year?

Lee worked long and hard to install computerized statistics. We could generate volumes of statistical pages with any kind of information you could ever want to know, including how different players perform in different situations. Nobody cared, so we went back to doing them by hand. Now all statistics are kept by computer because baseball teams need "pages of statistics with any kind of information you could ever want to know, including how different players perform . . ."

When July 4th was the worst drawing day of the season, we were the first to have a giant fireworks show following the game. It seems like old hat now, but we thought we were going to blow up the city then. Now, fireworks on July 4th are standard in every big-league stadium.

We were also the first to sell Bat Day to a sponsor. We sold it to Burger King, and baseball traditionalists were outraged that we'd prostitute the game by commercializing the promotional giveaways. Now every promotional giveaway day is sponsored, but, again, the only credit we got was for profaning a tradition.

Granted, some of our innovations didn't catch on. The calliope in center field never replaced the organ as a ballpark standard, nor did a chimpanzee sweeping the bases between innings displace many grounds-crew jobs. But we thought we deserved a little glory.

Even our mascot was the best known in baseball, if not the most respected. But that didn't come easily, either. We tried to find an Indian to dance in centerfield when the Braves hit a home run. The best we could do was a pudgy Boy Scout with a fancy chief's headdress. We had a radio contest and came up with a great name — Chief Noc-A-Homa — but our Boy Scout just didn't match the quality of the name.

We looked for alternatives. A sixty-foot mechanical Indian

was built behind the right-field fence. The plan was that each time the Braves hit a home run the Indian would wave the tomahawk in his right hand while his head turned back and forth with his eyes blinking. It sounds a lot better than it really was. First, the electrical connections were tricky. The Indian would sometimes wave and blink on its own. The red light bulbs in its eyes kept burning out, and it's not easy to climb a sixty-foot Indian to change light bulbs. Also, being made of painted styrofoam, our Indian lost a little more of whatever it had of its good looks each time a baseball hit it, and it became the primary target for home runs during batting practice. Finally, its head kept getting stuck facing backwards. Its name was "Big Victor," and that didn't help either.

"Big Victor" became a Braves memory after one season. He now lives in front of a general store someplace in north Georgia.

It was back to Noc-A-Homa as our not-so-great first-string mascot when one day, unannounced, a real Indian named Levi Walker walked into our offices. There was never a better fit between employee and employment. Levi became Noc-A-Homa not just at games but every moment of his life. He built his own teepee in left field. He made his own clothes. Sometimes we'd have him ride a horse around the field; sometimes he would swallow burning torches and blow flames from his mouth on the pitcher's mound . . . things only a real chief can do.

One season he circled the field each game in a Model A Ford for a bread sponsor. Another season he fired a Civil War-era cannon each time the Braves hit a homer, a salute that was stopped when a fan in the stands was hit by the wad from the cannon.

Noc-A-Homa was the source of a lot of fun, too. Our players would sneak up to his teepee platform and tie the shoelaces of his moccasins to a nail; opposing players would throw a cooler of ice water on him as he raced across the field to lead the Braves out of the dugout before a game. He always enjoyed getting into it with the visiting team's bullpen. They'd tackle him as he ran across the field one night, and the next night he'd

Chief Noc-A-Homa and friends outside the teepee.

bring a fire extinguisher and chase them away.

Once he made the national news when his teepee burned down during a game. We never found out why it caught fire, but the visiting pitchers were the logical suspects. Another time his smoke bomb backfired. It was supposed to shoot smoke through the top of his teepee whenever a Brave homered, but this time it smothered the field in smoke and delayed the game for a half-hour.

Twice the team removed his teepee from the stadium when it came time to install the Falcons' temporary seating at the beginning of the football season. Both times the team went into long losing streaks. The presence of Chief Noc-A-Homa and his teepee apparently brought the team what little luck it had.

We were never very fair to Noc-A-Homa. For fifty dollars a game he was our mascot full-time. For a while we put him on the regular office payroll, but he was impossible to manage. Once he arrived late at a banquet where new Georgia Tech football coach Bill Fulcher was the featured speaker. Coach

Fulcher was already starting his talk when Noc snuck up behind him on stage and let out a war whoop in his ear. The stunned coach sat down and never said another word the entire night. He never won another game in his coaching career either, for that matter.

We were always trying to find the right off-season job for Noc-A-Homa. If he couldn't work for the team full-time, we could at least help him find something else to support his family. Once he came to my office and gave me his new business card. He had become a partner in a company called "Three Boys Inc." — tax advisors. I choked at the thought of Noc preparing someone's taxes but asked him how he got into it. "It's a simple concept," he explained. "We have three partners — a white man, a black man, and an Indian — so we can offer a client whatever color tax consultant he needs — red, white, or black." The business never took off the way he hoped.

As Noc-A-Homa was struggling to support his family, I had the job of fending off his annual mascot salary demands. When it became evident to him he couldn't get more money, he started negotiating for fringe benefits. Our negotiations started being leaked to the newspapers (I suspect by the Chief), and he would play his leverage for all it was worth. Each year Noc held out for a little more, and before too long he had carpeting in the teepee, a television in the teepee, air conditioning, a refrigerator, a totem pole, lounge chairs, and finally even an Indian princess to spend the games with him.

Noc was a piece of work.

Finally, as with all great Braves stars, a new five-year plan for improvement included eliminating Chief Noc-A-Homa as the team's mascot. He was replaced by a kid in a giant foam Indian head and a fuzzball-like creature named "Rally." Both have since been canned. But Noc-A-Homa remains one of the greatest of the former Braves. He was frequently the most entertaining performer.

5

AN ALL-STAR YEAR

Lee Walburn and I were full of anticipation when the 1972 season got underway. The team was playing in new uniforms that we had hired local Atlanta artist Wayland Moore to help us design. It would be the start of a new look and a new era for the Braves. The home uniforms were white knits with big royal blue sleeves and a red, white, and blue feather on each shoulder. On the road, the shirts were bright blue, something baseball had never seen. The caps were blue with white fronts, and we used a lower-case cursive "a" to stand for Atlanta. But our pride was our batting helmet—blue with a flare of white from the bill to the peak of the crown. Some people said they looked like softball uniforms, but we were certain it was the baseball uniform of the future. We were ahead of our time.

We put that red, white, and blue feather design on everything. It was on the tops of the dugouts, across on the batters' circles, and throughout the pages of the game programs. The feather would replace what we considered the fruity-looking laughing Indian head that had served for years as the Braves' emblem. This was our mark on baseball.

Wayland Moore gave us something no other team had, an artist right in our offices who did all our work for free. We traded him office space at the stadium for his artwork. Lee and I took full advantage of having him around. We put his artwork on everything from our program covers to center field.

His speed amazed me as much as his talent. One time a woman came by our office to commission him to paint a golf scene for her husband. Wayland pleaded that he was so busy preparing for an upcoming art show that he wouldn't have time. She begged and he raised his price tag, finally agreeing to "work it in" somehow in the next couple of weeks. When the morning the painting was due arrived, I went to Wayland's office to see how it looked. He had forgotten to do it. Unperplexed, he whipped out a canvas and a few brushes, and the painting was complete by the time the woman arrived to pick it up a couple of hours later. She thought he'd been working on it for days.

Wayland himself was a work of art. Once, when the University of Alabama was playing in the Sugar Bowl in New Orleans, Wayland supplied a painting of the Alabama team in action to a Bourbon Street art gallery. The gallery operator called when a customer complained that the star quarterback in Wayland's painting was wearing the wrong number. Wayland had the gallery operator ship the painting back to Atlanta on a plane. I went with him to the airport, where he pulled out his paints, changed the uniform number, and shipped the painting back to be sold.

Wayland's new Braves logo was everywhere in 1972, even right in the middle of the circle that formed the larger logo for the 1972 All-Star Game, where it was surrounded by our theme for the season, "It's an All-Star Year." That's right: Atlanta had been selected to host baseball's 1972 All-Star Game. Lee had taken me with him to the 1971 game in Detroit, and we had studied hard. We would have more hospitality, more pageantry, a better game program, nicer souvenirs, better press accommodations than any sports event in history. That was our plan.

For me the prospect was almost overwhelming, but Lee was an old hand. He had been to virtually every big-time event from the Super Bowl to the World Series. He knew exactly what to do. And I was ready to help.

Two weeks into the season Lee came to me with staggering news. He was quitting the Braves to go to work for a local public relations firm, Ball & Cohn. I'd never heard of Ball & Cohn, but Lee said it was an opportunity he couldn't overlook. If things went right, he had a chance to make as much as $30,000 a year, and he could work a lifetime at the Braves and never reach a figure like that. I could understand how he couldn't pass up the new job, but I felt left in the lurch. In the first place, I had no guarantee that I would be asked to replace him as the Braves PR director. And second, if I got the job, I wasn't sure I'd have any idea what to do.

While Lee had been working to get ready for the All-Star Game, I had been struggling with the details of setting up the season's promotions for the stadium. I'd gotten a real deal on caps for Cap Day, even if they looked a little rattier than any caps I'd seen before and had felt letters pasted on the front. I'd gotten a deal. The T-shirts seemed a little snug, and the supplier wasn't sure they'd arrive in time for the T-shirt Day game. And the helmets with the new white flare were on order, but there was no assurance they could even be made. The helmet company was experimenting with ways to paint them. They had to find a way. After all, Helmet Day was already on the printed schedule.

I didn't have time to deal with anything else. What a time for Lee to leave. A couple of days after his announcement, Bill Bartholomay told me I would be Lee's replacement. I had the job. And with it came a raise from $11,000 to $13,000. He told me I was now in charge, the leader. My personality, he said, would be reflected in everything we did as an organization. That was a scary thought. I was notorious for going to Lee daily with a hundred wild things I wanted to do, but he would keep me in line. Now the restraint would have to be self-imposed.

In fact, I had been going to Lee with my ideas and problems ever since I started working for the Braves as a college freshman. We all went to Lee when we needed something. I quickly found out that part of the new job was that people would now be coming to me. Joyce Pruett was a small, nervous woman who worked in our public relations department. She was an efficient, diligent worker. Soon she was coming to me regularly to complain about working with Madaline Casey. Madaline was a tall, tough blonde in the same department and was also an effective worker. Madaline then started coming to me to complain about Joyce. At first I tried to talk them through their problems each visit, but finally I told them they needed to meet with each other and work out their differences. One day I heard slamming against walls and screaming in the back office. I found Joyce and Madaline brawling on the floor. I had a lot to learn about managing people.

Hosting the All-Star Game was my leading challenge, though. Lee had already lined up the support we needed to do things right. Atlanta companies Coca-Cola and Delta Air Lines and the Atlanta Chamber of Commerce pitched in money to add to the inadequate $40,000 contributed by Major League Baseball for hospitality at the game. When the baseball officials arrived in Atlanta on Sunday before the Tuesday-night game, they were picked up at the airport in cars provided by local car dealers and driven by volunteers. They were taken to the Atlanta Marriott for a big Sunday-night party. There was a breakfast Monday morning. The players were featured at the All-Star Luncheon on Monday. Monday night a Southern Plantation banquet was scheduled. On Tuesday, another breakfast and luncheon were on the agenda, and then before the game, a beer garden was set up at the stadium for officials and press.

We had a great program scheduled. Everything first class. And I was careful to live by the long-established commandment that Lee and I had discovered the year before: "No women allowed."

I was amazed with myself. I not only had the whole thing organized, but I had plenty of backup and extra security. Not only would there be no women; there would be no gate-crashers of any gender. We were ready.

As the Sunday-night party was about to get started, I was briefing the security guard at the door to the ballroom when my wife Susan arrived. I was telling her she couldn't go to the official hospitality event and would have to wait outside for me when Bill Lucas showed up at the door. As Susan was walking away, Bill, a black man, grabbed her arm and said, "Let's go have a drink." Susan responded by saying she couldn't go in, it was stag only. Bill said, "Look, my people weren't allowed to enter nice places for years, either. Come on, someone's got to be the first woman to integrate baseball." And the two of them walked in.

All hell broke loose. Commissioner Bowie Kuhn and National League President Warren Giles met with me to determine what I should do to correct the situation before other baseball officials arrived. After all, they would have their wives with them, and we would have to get the problem resolved so they wouldn't try to get in. I was at a loss for words since I didn't exactly understand the seriousness of the offense in the first place. But it was already too late. With Susan in the door, all the other baseball executives' wives—wives who had gone to All-Star Games for years and had always been excluded from the hospitality events—had already crashed the party, too. The wives were in revolt, and no one in baseball officialdom seemed any too happy.

Resigned, but doing a slow burn, baseball executives went to the hospitality functions accompanied by their brazen wives and girlfriends. They had been sorely violated, but they adapted as best they could. Then a miracle happened, one that probably saved my career. One of the wives approached the conductor of the orchestra playing at the dinner the night before the game and asked him if he could play some dance music. Suddenly the official men and illegal women started dancing. It even looked like they were having fun.

At the next night's post-game party, people were sitting on the floor in big circles, singing and telling stories. It was as if women had always been part of the festivities. I was saved. And women have been invited ever since.

As if one major transgression weren't enough, we screwed up the All-Star Game press box, too. Atlanta was new to the big leagues, and our Baseball Writers Association chapter was unaware of the other cardinal rule that Lee and I had dis-covered the year before: only writers — absolutely no broadcasters — were to be assigned seats in the press box.

But it was too late, and there was nothing we could do. The credentials were already given out and seats assigned. The dreaded broadcasters would be there. There would probably be a big brouhaha. Saved again. There were only about a hundred members of the Baseball Writers Association cover-ing the game out of a total of five hundred writers and broad-casters. Half the Association members never understood why broadcasters weren't allowed in the first place. After a brief confrontation and pointed reprimand (for me), the game went on, writers and broadcasters actually sitting together at the same tables. Baseball wasn't as quick to accept broadcasters in the press box as it was to accept women at its parties, but the first step was taken.

The All-Star Game itself was an amazing event for Atlanta. Every seat was filled on a night that sparkled with excitement. I lost my temper briefly when Chief Noc-A-Homa showed up in a new turquoise polyester Indian outfit, which I felt was far too non-Indian for such a big event. I sent him home to change into his official Chief togs, and he was back in plenty of time for the game. Then, with the game about to begin, I learned that I was responsible for yet another All-Star Game first. When the umpires entered the field for the start of the game, they noticed we had the All-Star Game logo painted in a huge circle that took up most of the outfield. It was an idea I got from NFL games which always had logos painted on their field. Apparently that, too, had never been done in baseball and was not covered in the ground rules for the game. It presented a problem, but the options were few. Either play the game or face the embarrassment of being the first game in baseball history cancelled due to painted grass. They played.

We were a little overzealous at times during the game. Hometown hero Hank Aaron won the All-Star Game Most Valuable Player balloting when we decided to take the vote at the end of the sixth inning after the National League had jumped ahead on his home run. But the team fell behind again and came back to win on a Joe Morgan homer. We took a revote, and the record book now shows Morgan as the award winner.

Except for the All-Star Game, the 1972 season turned out to be reasonably uneventful for both me and the Braves. I fought my way through my new job, and the Braves fought their way to a fourth-place finish, firing manager Luman Harris and hiring former Braves great Eddie Mathews along the way. Hank Aaron hit thirty-four more home runs, putting himself just forty-one short of Babe Ruth's lifetime record of 714.

6

THE TEAM THAT CHASED BABE RUTH

Two games remained in the 1973 season. The Braves were in fifth place and had been well out of the pennant race for months. The day was September 29, and only about 7,500 fans were watching the Braves play the Houston Astros in a game that meant nothing. Henry Louis Aaron stepped up to the plate and swatted his fortieth home run of the season. That left him just one short of the Babe, with one game left in the season. It also caused the greatest rush on tickets I've ever seen.

Aaron had created the majority of excitement for the 1973 team. He entered the season within striking distance of Babe Ruth's all-time career home run record, and with a brigade of writers and broadcasters following him constantly, it appeared he would finish the season with thirty-nine, two homers short. In a normal year, thirty-nine homers would lead the league. This season it didn't even lead the team. Aaron ranked third behind teammates Dave Johnson (forty-three) and Darrell Evans (forty-one).

This was before there was such thing as computerized tickets, so the only place to purchase a ticket to the next game was at the stadium. Between the fifth inning of that Saturday-night game and two o'clock the next day, 40,000 tickets were sold.

Sunday, September 30, was rainy and cold. Hank went to

bat four times that day. Each time the crowd rose to its feet in anticipation, but he didn't hit the home run. In his final time at bat, he popped up to second baseman Tommy Helms, and one of the greatest tributes ever paid to any athlete gradually started to take place — spontaneously.

A thirty-nine-year-old man, who had just disappointed a crowd that had jammed the stadium to see him hit a home run, jogged slowly to his spot in left field. Gradually the applause of the fans started building, and soon 40,517 people were on their feet cheering. They remained on their feet applauding for more than five minutes while a baseball legend stood alone in the outfield, tipping his cap in return for the adulation. The crowd cheered and cheered. It was the most touching moment I've ever witnessed in sports.

The 1973 Braves had a lot of hitting and very little pitching. But if there was one overriding cause of their fifth-place finish, it may have been the distraction of accompanying Hank Aaron on his home run chase. Hundreds of writers and thousands of fans showed up wherever the team did. Everyone was interested in just one performer. Never have twenty-four players been so ignored with so much media around. If another player was asked a question by a writer, it was, "What's it been like playing with Hank Aaron?"

It was the same thing over and over everywhere they went. The players heard Hank asked every possible question and knew every answer. I knew Hank's answers so well that I stood in for him with a group of Japanese writers who interviewed me at a makeshift press conference in the dugout of Dodger Stadium. The writers from Japan asked me to pretend I was Hank. They asked me the questions through an interpreter, and I answered them with what I thought Hank would say. I assume no one back home in Tokyo ever knew any difference. They had interviewed Hank Aaron.

The 1973 season was a traveling circus for the entire team. Eddie Mathews was the Braves' manager that year. As a player, he had been a fixture at third base for the Braves for fifteen seasons. He was an authority on home-run hitting himself, having led the league twice and sharing the career home-run record for teammates with Aaron. As a player he had been traded after the 1966 season for Houston's Dave Nicholson, but he came back as a coach for the team in 1970. He was named manager in 1972.

Mathews was still enormously popular in Atlanta. His days as a young third-baseman for the old minor-league Atlanta Crackers had never been forgotten. He had youthful, All-American looks and the perfect athletic build, and he was notorious for having fought baseballs on the infield until he taught himself to play third base. He worked hard. He also played hard.

Mathews was a heavy drinker and legendary fighter, on and off the field. At most times he was quiet and almost shy, but his hot temper could blow at any moment with the slightest provocation . . . sometimes with no provocation at all. His bad side showed frequently, but he was also noted for backing his friends and caring about his players. If you knew Eddie, you soon learned how to handle yourself in a fight, either with him or against him. It came with the territory.

Eddie knew how to manage a baseball team. Most big-league teams are over-managed and under-led. Eddie had the right combination. When Sparky Anderson was managing the Cincinnati Reds, I overheard Johnny Bench tell him, "Sparky, your mother carried you for nine months. We've been carrying you for three seasons." The great baseball managers seem to be the ones who let the players do their jobs with as little interference as possible. That was Eddie's approach to the game. He let his horses run. Eddie also protected Hank.

It's impossible to fully explain what the Braves went through that year. They were swarmed everywhere; fans acted as if a rock star were coming to town. Security guards had to force a path through the crowds at hotels just to get the Braves to their buses. They would register Hank in one hotel room and have him stay in another. It was the only way he could have any privacy.

That '73 team had a rainbow of colorful characters. If Aaron was the king, Ralph Garr was the court jester. Garr was a young black outfielder from Ruston, Louisiana. Bright-eyed, always happy, and rubber-faced, he made it to the big leagues on his batting. He came close to hitting .400 in the minor leagues and led the National League in 1971, hitting .343. He followed with .325 the next year—his first two full seasons in the major leagues.

After leading the league his first year, Garr summoned the nerve to ask for a raise, from the big-league minimum salary of $12,500 to $21,000. He had to settle for $17,500. Those days, leading the league in batting wasn't enough to justify a big raise.

Ralph was called "Gator" by his teammates because of his Louisiana home, and his style of play was electrifying. He'd swing at anything. No pitch was out of his strike zone, and he was probably the fastest player in the league. Since he was a left-handed hitter, just about anything hit on the ground was a base hit. The frequency of his infield hits and his quick burst of speed to first base prompted fans to nickname him "Road Runner."

He had a knack for drawing analogies that made his personality just as colorful as his baseball. In the locker room the players would sit in a circle around him. Ralph would always be perched next to his hero, whom he always addressed as "Mr. Aaron."

"When you hit the ball hard, that's talent," he'd say. "When nobody catches it, that's luck."

"It doesn't matter what color somebody's skin is," he'd declare. "Everybody bleeds red."

He'd tell stories about growing up playing ball with his boyhood friend, Lee Chester Peavey. Ralph described Lee Chester as the greatest hitter he had ever seen—much better than Ralph. Both had long since left Louisiana, but Ralph noted that the distance between them now couldn't be measured in miles. Lee Chester was the bellhop at the hotel where the Braves stayed when they played in Houston.

Ralph would candidly admit the good fortune that gave him

the chance to be in the big leagues, the fate that eluded Lee Chester. Ralph was recruited out of high school by the coach of the Grambling University baseball team. The coach was a remarkable man who changed the lives of many young black athletes, who influenced them not just to play baseball but to achieve other great things in their lives. The coach was Ralph Waldo Emerson Jones, the world's only baseball coach and college president.

President Jones talked with affection about Ralph Garr, too. He told the story of a youngster coming out of the backwoods of Cajun country with little confidence and badly in need of dental work. Coach Jones had Ralph's teeth fixed and President Jones approved the money to have it done. President-Coach Jones nurtured Ralph through college and was one of his biggest fans.

Hank played leftfield, Ralph right, and Ralph's best friend, Dusty Baker, was in center. Dusty was the antithesis of Ralph. Tall, slender, and quiet, he possessed an easy smile and friendly nature. Each off-season I would hire three or four players to make speeches and appearances for the Braves. Ralph and Dusty did it one year and always went as a duo. They could charm any group of hostile fans. They always showed up on time and always pleased the crowd.

Only once did I ever have a complaint—the day they were supposed to appear in a circus parade. They didn't show up and the promoter was furious. When I got back to my office after lunch that day, Ralph and Dusty were waiting.

"You mad at us, boss?" Ralph asked.

"Why shouldn't I be?" I replied.

The two explained how they had shown up for the start of the parade that morning and were on a street corner downtown when a man told them to go with him. He took them to a parking lot full of elephants.

"He took a stick and knocked that elephant on the trunk, and then he told me to climb up its nose, sit on its head, and hang on to its ears and ride that elephant down the street," Ralph explained. "I thought about it for a minute and was about to do it for you, boss," he continued. "But I saw this vision of myself riding an elephant when a kid jumped out of the crowd and threw a firecracker under its feet."

"We just couldn't go through with it," they apologized.

On any other team, Dusty would have been the big star that year. He hit more than twenty homers and had a .288 batting average. But that kind of year was virtually overlooked on a team with three forty-plus homer-hitters, one chasing Babe Ruth.

The young third baseman on the team was Darrell Evans. He was strong and serious. He reminded fans of Mathews not just because of his home-run power but also because he struggled with the same intensity to master fielding third base. A lot of baseballs bounced off his chest. He went on from the Braves to become the only player ever to hit more than a hundred home runs on three different teams. Evans, like Baker, was a very quiet man.

Most players seemed to want the team's second baseman, Davey Johnson, to be quiet, too. Johnson was nearing the end of his playing career and had never hit more than eighteen home runs in a season. His forty-three during the 1973 season was completely unexpected. As a player, he was having a career year. As a personality, he was what the players called a "clubhouse lawyer." He knew the answers to all questions, no matter what the subject matter. His temperament resembled tennis's John McEnroe; he was an overgrown crybaby who wore on the nerves of everybody else on the team.

Daily statistics sheets were distributed before every game, updating the batting and pitching for the season. To my knowledge, no other player paid much attention to the stat sheets. Davey would challenge them every game. If persuasion and lobbying could get a player an extra hit, Johnson would have led the league in hitting every year.

The shortstop on the field with Johnson was Marty Perez, a slightly built and not particularly gifted player whose tenacity kept him in the game for ten big-league seasons. Latin short-stops are famous for showing up in the minor leagues without knowing a word of English, but Marty was Hispanic in heritage only. He was born and bred in California and hadn't the slightest hint of a Spanish accent. He didn't fit the stereotype. For a shortstop, he was a solid hitter, batting .250 for the season while scoring sixty-six runs and driving in fifty-seven. He was more natural at second base than shortstop, but Johnson had second locked up. Perez was twenty-seven but looked like a high-school freshman. He was always smiling and friendly, which also contributed to his long career. He was a good man to have on a team.

Catcher Johnny Oates was another "good man" with no remarkable skills. He hit under .250 but stayed in the major league for eleven seasons with five different teams. In baseball, nice guys may finish last but they at least stay on the team.

Mike Lum, the only Hawaiian in baseball, was the first baseman. It wasn't his natural position, but then, neither was the outfield. He wasn't fast, he wasn't strong, he couldn't hit with power or for particularly high average. He was reliable if not notable. He hit .294 and drove in eighty-two runs that year, the best season of his fifteen in the majors.

The pitching staff was led by red-haired right-hander Carl Morton, called "Carl Perfect Pitch" by the players. He was a serious student of pitching, and, in fact, he seemed totally serious about everything he did. He even read the safety instructions along with the flight attendant before every plane trip. When he had a party at his house one night, he carefully explained to the guests how he had specially ordered every piece of furniture, every piece of trim, and every piece of tile in the entire place. Each item had been carefully selected to match everything else. His wife Sandy had suffered a nervous breakdown earlier that year, which didn't surprise any of us after Carl's tour of the house. He was always perfectly groomed and precisely dressed, never allowing the least imperfection. Even when he was pitching a poor game, Carl was always under control. He just got hit.

Morton led the staff with fifteen wins in 1973, and Phil

Niekro followed with thirteen, one of which was the only no-hitter of his long career—and the only one in Atlanta Braves history. This was the first of two seasons that Phil and brother Joe were on the same team. Joe was a relief pitcher on the Braves and won just two games. Both threw the knuckleball, the odd pitch taught them by their father. They were two of only three knuckleballers in the league, the third being the Cubs' Burt Hooten.

Phil was well on his way to Hall of Fame status by 1973. Having Joe on the team with him was regarded more as nepotism than as smart baseball. It wasn't until Joe left the Braves that he re-established himself as a starter and won 163 of his 221 career victories. While Phil never made it to a World Series, Joe pitched in one for the Twins in 1987, the season before his last.

If it seems all the Braves had good seasons in 1973, it makes it all the more amazing that the team finished with a 76-85 record, good for fifth place in the six-team Western Division. Something must have gone wrong.

To begin with, starting pitcher Ron Reed, who stood six-foot seven-inches tall and had played basketball for the Detroit Pistons, won only four and lost eleven games for the season. Reed was in his eighth season as a Brave and had been selected an All-Star in 1969, when the team won the division. He was a big, blue-eyed, curly-haired blonde from Indiana. If there had been an All-Star wife team, Julie Reed would have made it. She was a beautiful, long-haired blonde, who always drew appreciative ogling from the press box when she'd walk to and from the wives seating area behind home plate. She also upheld baseball's tradition for the best-looking wife on a team: she was popular with the players and front office but ignored by the other wives. There was as much politics among the wives as among the players.

Another starting pitcher, Pat Dobson, won only three games. Dobson had been a twenty-game winner for Baltimore before being traded to the Braves, and he became a nineteen-game winner for the Yankees after leaving Atlanta, but he never could win in a Braves uniform.

The relief pitching on the team was also weak. Danny Frisella, a right-handed relief ace obtained in a trade from the Mets, appeared in forty-two games but managed only one win and eighteen saves with a 4.20 ERA. Danny and Pam Frisella always told me they wanted to introduce me to a little-known pitcher friend of theirs who they said looked and talked just like me. His name was Nolan Ryan.

In a morbid oddity, both the top starting pitcher and the top relief pitcher for the 1973 Braves died tragically as young men. Frisella was killed in 1977 in a dune buggy accident. Morton died of a heart attack after jogging in 1983.

I thought the 1973 Braves, the team that participated with Hank Aaron in his home run chase, was the most cohesive and interesting of the Braves' quarter-century. They were there when the home run chase fell one short at the end of the season, and most of them were still in place on opening day of 1974 when the chase resumed.

But the team was changed drastically midway into the 1974 season. Eddie Mathews was fired for stopping the team bus on the way to a game to buy beer. The players, who loved and respected Eddie, were extremely upset, and the fans were equally outraged, but as always, management thought it was the right thing to do. The Braves had a winning record when he was fired. The next season they fell to 67-94 and finished 40½ games out of first.

7

THE VALUE OF
A GOLDEN HAMMER

Daniel J. Donahue was president of the Atlanta Braves in 1974 when Hank Aaron set the all-time home-run record. Mr. Donahue was a rotund, graying man in his fifties. He had been assigned by the team's owners in Chicago to tighten up the ship. The Braves had been floundering on the field and attendance was poor. It was his job to straighten things out and get them back on track.

I liked Mr. Donahue. He'd puff on his cigar and explain to me the complexities of American business. One day we went to a stockbroker's office. It was neat and clean. He told me the best stockbrokers had messy offices with old furniture. Mr. Donahue said it, so I believed it. He analyzed anything and everything, and he seemed to be having his best time when he was talking about the most complicated financial workings of the business world and knew I wasn't understanding a thing he said.

He was also president of Atlanta/LaSalle Corporation, the parent company of the Braves. He and a younger Ivy League-type wheeler-dealer named Peter Foley would analyze companies and put together plans to go buy them. They were big-time deal-makers. When they'd complete a deal, they'd have me write a press release to announce it to the news media. Whatever phrases I'd use in the release to explain what had taken place would always have to be changed. I was lost in the business mumbo jumbo of "acquired," "bought," "merged," or whatever. I couldn't figure out the difference. But I knew Mr. Donahue knew.

On November 2, 1974, less than seven months after Aaron broke Ruth's record, Mr. Donahue called me to his office. What he told me was a shock. The Braves had traded Hank Aaron to the Milwaukee Brewers for two players I'd never heard of—Dave May and Roger Alexander.

I was waiting for the explanation. He told me Hank was past his prime as a player, having hit only twenty home runs with just sixty-nine RBI during the record-breaking season. Hank's salary, he noted, was more than $100,000 a year, far too much for any ballplayer. "Only chief executive officers of major corporations should be paid that much," he declared. "Men who went to college deserve big salaries, but no athlete is worth a hundred thousand dollars."

The Braves were not willing to pay Aaron the salary. The Brewers were. It was that simple. Hank was gone.

Donald Davidson told me that Hank wanted to retire as a player and go to work in the Braves' office but wanted $80,000 a year. If it was ridiculous to pay Hank $100,000 as a player, Donald emphasized, it would be insane to pay any baseball executive $80,000. Hank, Donald believed, had a false sense of reality.

The whole situation baffled me. Mr. Donahue was wise, I thought, about a lot of important things, but he wasn't wise in the ways of baseball. It just didn't make sense to trade Hank Aaron. He belonged in a Braves uniform. He was an institution. His absence would cut the heart out of the organization. I stated my case and lost. I was absolutely wrong, I was told.

I met Hank for the first time when I was working for the Braves in college. Before each game, it was my job to go to the clubhouse to get autographs and fulfill a myriad of requests that fans or office people had for the players. For every request for anyone else, there were three or four for Hank. He was

Atlanta Brave-of-all-time Henry Aaron

always perfectly gracious and accommodating. Hank Aaron was one of the most genuinely nice people I had ever met.

For all the credit he received for setting baseball's hitting records, one of the most impressive roles he played was his handling of his status as the first black superstar in the South. When the Braves moved to Atlanta from Milwaukee, only whites played major-college football and basketball at southern schools. Atlanta had no National Football League or National Basketball Association team, and the only baseball was minor league. Blacks had been playing for the Atlanta Crackers for a half-dozen years, and Dave Ricketts and Johnny Lewis later played for the Cards. But the Braves' move to the South coincided with the heightening of the civil rights movement.

Atlanta was the focal point of the movement, home of all its most visible leaders. As the nation's sports attention focused on the advent of major league baseball in Atlanta, the news media were watching the city for other reasons.

The atmosphere was uncomfortable. Even those whites and blacks who were at peace with the idea of integration had never been through it before. White Atlantans like me had never been to school with blacks, but we had no trouble with that idea. We knew blacks deserved equal rights, and schools and restaurants were fine. Sports were somehow different. Back when we were in high school, people were still telling us blacks would bite or scratch in football, and that if they sweated on us, it would burn our skin. We knew those things were ridiculous, but the idea of blacks playing sports against whites still made us uneasy.

The first integrated high-school football game in Atlanta was between all-white Northside High and all-black Washington High, the year after I graduated. I was at the game, and the atmosphere was tense. One side of the stadium was filled with whites and the other with blacks. The rumor was that there would be violence. As best I could tell, no one seemed to be looking for trouble, but everyone was aware of the possibility.

At halftime, the Northside band played first and left the field. Then came time for the Washington band's performance. The marchers walked slowly and deliberately, every step exaggerated, from the end zone corner down the opposite sideline from where we were sitting. Finally, the entire sideline was filled with a single file of black band members standing as if they were frozen. Our perplexity grew while they stood motionless for what seemed like minutes. Then, in an explosion of drums, the band took off, high-stepping right towards us like a charging army. The announcer shouted on the public address system, "Look out white folks, here they come!" At first, everybody in the all-white stands started to jump up and run for their lives, but then we all laughed at our own reaction and settled back to enjoy a great halftime show. The tension was broken, but the experience showed that the South wasn't yet used to integration on the sports field when the Braves arrived.

In 1966, race riots broke out in Atlanta, and young, militant blacks were shouting, "Burn, baby, burn." Stokely Carmichael coined the term "Black Power." The same Mayor Ivan Allen, Jr., who was credited with landing the Braves for Atlanta, was now standing on the tops of cars in the midst of chaos attempting to calm racial tensions.

Through it all, Hank Aaron calmly played his superb brand of big-league baseball. One weekend in 1967, more than 100,000 mostly white fans watched the Braves and Cardinals play baseball at the stadium while thousands of blacks demonstrated just blocks away. Aaron handled his job with such sensitivity that virtually no one noticed the key role he was playing. He led in the civil rights movement by example. He was the picture of dignity and goodwill.

Once the FBI stationed agents at the gates of the stadium to check fans as they entered. The Braves were playing the Dodgers, and there was a warning that a sniper might be at the game. Baseball was played that day, and Hank, though he knew of the threat, was on the field and never said a word.

As the pressures of the civil rights movement subsided, the

pressures of the home-run chase began. Hank was the center of the storm. On the road he couldn't leave his hotel room without being swarmed by fans. And not all of them were friendly. One night in Los Angeles, for instance, Hank joined a group of us sitting around a table in the hotel bar. Immediately people started lining up for autographs. Eventually, a man sitting across the room walked up to Hank and challenged him. "You think you're better than the rest of us!" he charged. Then the man starting shoving Hank, and we had to pull him away. Hank simply retreated back to his room, apologizing to us for "causing the problem." The man was right on one point: Hank was better than the rest of us. No one could have handled the job of role model as well as he did.

The sports media became obsessed with Aaron's quest for the home-run record. As he got closer, the number of media people traveling with the team increased to presidential proportions. Planes of writers and broadcasters would trail the Braves on the road, and a flock of writers would surround Hank everywhere he went. When he arrived at the ballpark before each game, the reporters were waiting. He'd go through a series of prearranged interviews for the first couple of hours and then retreat to the trainer's room to rest for a while before batting practice. Back outside, a long line of fans would be waiting for autographs and pictures.

Before almost every game there was a special presentation to Hank on the field. Civic organizations, foundations, communities, and politicians wanted to present trophies or plaques to him for a variety of causes, but it seemed that most of them just wanted to get their pictures taken with him. Hank would graciously accept the awards, smile, and thank them. He was always patient.

His most relaxing time was during the games. He would sit in the dugout or play in the outfield for nine innings without intrusion from the outside world. It was about the only peace and quiet he had. After each game a press-briefing room was set up with rows of chairs for about four hundred reporters and a table in front for Hank. He'd answer their questions until they were finished. Every single night.

For a couple of years the pressure on him built up to a phenomenal level, and my own involvement with Hank's daily life was not always enjoyable. I would set up his press interviews and host the post-game press conferences. I also arranged for youngsters to meet him before each game. The only person I could be sure would always be cooperative was Hank.

I'd get phone calls and letters each day from parents who wanted their children to meet Hank. Most would tell me their youngsters had serious illnesses and suggest that meeting Hank would bring happiness at a difficult time. So there would always be a line of youngsters in the dugout to meet him before every game. He would sign baseballs and have his photo made with each one.

With the pressures building on Hank, not to mention the trouble it was causing me, I suggested to him that we could easily eliminate the time with the youngsters. Meeting Hank was great for the ones who were really sick, but we were now having parents call and bring whole teams of kids who were supposed to be critically ill. It was getting out of hand, and there was no way to tell the real cases from the cheats. Hank instructed me to keep bringing the youngsters. He never stopped meeting with groups of kids before every game.

One day, several years after the home-run record was broken and Hank had retired as a player, I was stopped by a stranger in an airport. "You're Bob Hope, aren't you?" he asked. "You don't remember me," he noted correctly, "but you did me a favor years ago."

He explained he had called me several years earlier to arrange for his son to meet Hank Aaron. He and his family were traveling from Florida to New Orleans, where his son was having open-heart surgery. The family stopped in Atlanta to see the Braves play, he said, and I took them to the dugout where Hank signed a baseball for his son and posed for a photo. His son was thrilled, he told me. He then explained his son had died during the surgery.

"I can't tell you what it meant to us for the last few days of his life to be happy ones," he said.

That story says it all about Hank Aaron as a man. As great as he was as a player, he was never showy or self-important. He was a kind and gentle man who treated people with respect every day.

On the field Hank was the most perfect player I ever saw. Baseball was effortless for him. His wrists were so quick and strong that his home-run swing appeared deceptively easy. Curt Simmons, who pitched against Hank for the Cards and Cubs, said that trying to throw a fastball past Aaron was like trying to sneak the sunrise by a rooster.

His fielding was also a study in economy. Once, when Pete Rose was playing right field for the Reds against the Braves, a foul ball was hit deep along the first-base line. Rose gave chase, arms and legs flying wildly, and crashed into the fence in a valiant try for the catch. The ball fell to the ground just beyond the reach of his glove.

Aaron was playing right field for the Braves the next half inning when a foul ball was hit to the exact same spot. Aaron glided over to the fence, reached over, and caught it with what appeared to be routine effort. The crowd cheered loudly for Rose's fruitless effort and applauded courteously for Hank. He made it look too easy.

Aaron's greatest moment in the sun was accomplished in the same style. He tied Babe Ruth the first game of the 1974 season in Cincinnati and then gave Atlantans the thrill they wanted by breaking the record during the opening game in Atlanta that year.

Celebrities descended on Atlanta to see his moment. Pearl Bailey sang the national anthem. Sammy Davis, Jr., and Jimmy Carter were there. Hank's parents, children, and wife were on hand. The TV networks had been breaking into regular programming to show each of his at bats until he broke the record. The game was televised live to an audience of more than forty million and more than 50,000 saw it in person. Hundreds of reporters were on hand to cover it. Everyone went wild when he hit it. Two fans broke the security barrier to run with him around the bases. Fireworks exploded high above the stadium, and the game stopped for a half-hour ceremony on the field when he crossed the plate. Everything and everyone seemed out of control for a moment except, of course, Hank. He was in complete control.

Off the field Hank wasn't always perfect. Sometimes he'd refuse to participate in promotional events, particularly Camera Day, which required players to stand in the sun for an hour before the game while people took photos. Once he even started a fight of sorts. The *Atlanta Constitution* had run a photo of Hank's wife, Billye, along with a caption that offended her. Hank took it out on Frank Hyland, who had the misfortune of being the first sportswriter Hank saw that day. It was Georgia Agriculture Day at the stadium, and the players' lockers were filled with farm produce. Hanked reached for the first thing he could find and hit Frank in the face with a carton of strawberries. No one was injured, but the stature of the warriors combined with the oddity of the weapon made the "fight" front-page news across the nation the next day.

I asked Frank how he was doing the next day when he arrived at the park. "How would you feel if a legend hit you in the face with a carton of strawberries?" he answered sheepishly.

Hank was truly a legend. But because he played away from the limelight of New York and because he was a quiet man, he never achieved the commercial attention of Mickey Mantle, Willie Mays, Reggie Jackson, or any number of other baseball stars with lesser records. Hank, for instance, advertised Oh Henry candy bars, while Reggie Jackson had a candy bar named after him. But his stature is unmistakable. At the Goodwill Games in Seattle, seven-foot Wilt Chamberlain walked into the stands and hardly anyone noticed. Hank came in and sat next to Chamberlain and a buzz went through the crowd. After all, he is the greatest home-run hitter of all time.

After Hank retired, few took him seriously in his attempts to become baseball commissioner, general manager of a team, or a field manager. People were always quick to point out that breaking the home-run record didn't qualify him for those jobs. It was as if breaking the record was being held against him.

Hank finally rejoined the Braves as the team's farm director, pursuing his baseball career where he belongs, as a Brave.

8
SINKING FAST
TOWARDS LAST

Life without Hank Aaron proved to be just plain dull for the 1975 Braves, and the result was the least memorable season in Atlanta history. Only 534,000 people attended the home games, and we had to cheat to get that high. At the end of the year, we started buying free tickets from ourselves for twenty-five cents each and calling them paid admissions. The season was awful and we were groping for respectability in the midst of disaster.

We knew the team was bad, but the only real explanation for the dismal attendance, as far as we were concerned, was our ridiculous but lucrative television contract with a station we considered inferior for a big-league club. Ever since the team arrived from Milwaukee, twenty or so games a season had been televised on WSB TV, Atlanta's most prestigious station. It was the flagship of a network that stretched from Tennessee to Florida and west to Mississippi. WSB's general manager, a stately leader in the community named Don Eliot Heald, held a press conference during the 1972 season to reveal research that showed Braves games were the most-watched programming of the spring and summer months in Atlanta. The alliance between the Braves and WSB was strong and successful. It would surely last forever.

In January of 1973, the Braves announced that the games

were switching from WSB and would be televised on a struggling Atlanta UHF station, WTCG, Channel 17. This was a horrifying thought because there wasn't a soul in Atlanta who would admit to ever having watched Channel 17.

The new television deal with WTCG was a major step backwards in prestige even though it was described as a significant financial gain. WSB had paid about $200,000 to put the twenty games on television. Word was that WTCG would jump the number of televised games to sixty and pay $600,000 for the rights. Money or no money, it didn't seem right for a big-league team to be on a Mickey Mouse station with a reputation of showing only cartoons, old grade-D movies and 1950s television reruns. Some of us feared the Braves would be forgotten; we weren't even sure people could get the WTCG signal on their TV sets. Others feared everyone would see the televised games and sixty a year would prove beyond the saturation point. No one would come in person to see our games. After all, sixty free games on television is a lot of baseball.

When the Braves' contract was signed, WTCG had just changed its call letters from WJRJ, but the programming was pretty much the same. A new guy had taken over, and "WTCG" supposedly stood for "Watch this Channel Grow." It really stood for Turner Communications Group, named after Ted Turner, the man who ran it.

Working for a baseball team puts you in front of almost every important business person in a city, and I thought I knew virtually all of them. I had never heard of Ted Turner, and I couldn't find anyone else who had, either.

At the announcement of the TV deal, Dan Donahue briefed us about the station and its new operator. Turner was born in Cincinnati and came to Atlanta after running his father's billboard operation in Macon, Georgia. The "Turner" name now rang a bell. "Turner Advertising" was the nameplate on the bottom of every billboard in town. I had driven by the company's headquarters on Ashby Street, in one of the rougher, run-down sections of Atlanta, many times.

Turner had merged a couple of radio stations he owned

with Rice Broadcasting, which owned WJRJ, as his part of the deal to buy into WTCG. Since the station had been struggling anyway, they decided to change the name of the company to Turner Communications Corporation and change the call letters of the station at the same time. It gave them a fresh look. Jack Rice was still the major partner in the merger, but thirty-four-year-old Ted Turner was working to buy him out.

Jack Carlin, the Braves' director of broadcasting who arranged our TV deal with Turner, gave me more insight into the new guy. Ted was brash and bold and sometimes acted like an obnoxious drunk at a fraternity party. Jack said the Braves had taken Ted to the proverbial cleaners. Even if the station couldn't stay on the air, we would get our money — triple what we were paid in the past. The worst thing that could happen would be returning to WSB the next year.

Carlin was a cagey businessman. He knew Turner was taking a big chance, trying to do something big to put his station on the map. Jack seemed to like giving him that chance. UHF was a dirty word in television, and Turner thought the Braves might bring it respectability. Big-league baseball was one of the few kinds of programming that people tuned to regardless of the station. They would search out WTCG to watch the Braves — if, that is, they could pick up the TV signal.

The first time I met Ted Turner made me wonder even more what we had done to ourselves for a new TV deal. He was a thin, wiry man with a moustache, a big gap between his front teeth, and a big dimple on his chin. He looked a lot like Rhett Butler from *Gone with the Wind*, who I later suspected was his role model, but his frantic personality was far from that of the cool, unflappable Rhett. Turner's constant fidgeting made me nervous. We were sitting in the Braves' conference room, a half-dozen of us on the team's staff along with Turner and his chief Braves TV salesman, an unassuming man named Jim Thrash. Turner started talking and didn't stop the entire meeting. He stood on his chair, jumped up and down on the floor. He explained to us the way he sold television time. He didn't use slide shows or presentation books; he said those were just crutches. He said he talked advertisers into buying time. After watching the station, it seemed most of his talking was done to automobile dealers and record companies.

Turner told us he knew how to make things exciting, and he could help us with the Braves. If he ran the team, he said, he'd make the players real people. "Those guys are a bunch of stiffs," he screeched in the raspiest voice I'd never heard. "Nobody knows them. You need to make them real people. When people know they're real people they'll love them. Remember Joe Hardy in *Damn Yankees*. His poor old Washington team never won. But they had heart. People need to know the Braves have heart. The team should do a television commercial with all the players, the whole team, everyone of them singing 'You've got to have heart.'" Then he went on to sing the entire song.

Give me a break, I thought. Who is this nut?

After the meeting I heard a rumor that Turner had inherited his money when his father committed suicide, and it would only be a matter of time before he lost it all. I also heard the young Turner had saved his father's billboard company from the brink of bankruptcy and built it back to become the financial strength of an aspiring broadcast empire. I couldn't tell which was true. The latter proved to be the case.

"Jack," I asked Carlin after the meeting, "Have we got any chance at all of this thing working?" Jack didn't answer.

I learned what I could about Turner. He attended military school as a boy. He was an expert sailor and had won a lot of yachting races. He was planning to sail in the America's Cup, whatever that was. He attended Brown University and was kicked out just before graduation, either for burning down a homecoming float or for having a woman in his room. Nobody seemed to know which. I suspected both.

While at Brown, he studied classics, and even years after leaving school he was still prone to rattle off line after line of ancient literature with only the slightest provocation. His

father, who built the outdoor advertising business after growing up as the son of a Mississippi cotton farmer, was appalled
at Ted's choice of majors, but the disagreement was typical of
Turner's relationship with his dad. Ted worshipped his father
but had always struggled for his approval, from the time he
was sent off to a military boarding school until they worked
together in the billboard business.

Ted successfully built the billboard business after his father
died, and many felt he was a solid businessman on that basis.
But other ventures, like a shipbuilding company and a printing company, had failed, so other people were inclined to
discredit him. In fact, when he went to Atlanta's C & S Bank to
finance his television venture, the bank's president, Dick Kat-
tel, refused the loan and told him he'd go belly up. It was
difficult to judge quite what to think of Ted Turner.

The week after Turner signed the Braves' TV deal, Jack took
me over to visit WTCG's studios, a dilapidated converted production building on West Peachtree Street north of downtown
Atlanta. Jack pointed to the huge transmitter tower on the side
of the building and told me that when a friend pointed out to
Turner that it was the tallest televison tower in the world,
Turner bought it on the spot. "That's the way the guy is," he
noted. The tower was impressive, but the old tires strewn
around the base made it fit in better with the rest of the
station.

Ted and the tower were the only two things standing tall at
the station those days. The place was spartan and run-down.
A local sportswriter, following a tour of the facility, said he'd
seen nicer radio shacks in the navy. The TV sales staff was
deployed to the streets to hawk commercials that advertisers
could be sure almost no one would ever see. To motivate
them, Ted would stand on one of the old beat-up desks in the
cramped offices and give them a rousing pep-talk. They would
then charge out and sell more time on "Leave it to Beaver"
and "I Love Lucy."

Once, when Ted's other small station in Charlotte, North
Carolina, was about to go broke, he went on the air in a Jerry

Lewis-like telethon to raise money to keep the station alive. It worked, and Ted kept his fledgling empire struggling along by the skin of its teeth.

News wasn't a big deal at WTCG. The FCC required all stations to run a newscast, so the Channel 17 version was on at three in the morning. However, to save money, it was taped the previous afternoon. The night staff of the station consisted of one person who kept an old black-and-white film projector running the movies that played on the station all night long. The only break was the news. The anchor, Bill Tush, was occasionally joined by a German shepherd dog as co-anchor. On a typical night, his presentation of the latest news would be accentuated by a backdrop of King Kong climbing the buildings of the Atlanta skyline. The tone of the newscast was somewhere between "The David Letterman Show" and "Saturday Night Live." Humorous news may not have been what the world wanted, but it hardly mattered at three in the morning.

One day I was walking through the studio when Tush was taping his newscast for the next morning. I wadded up a piece of paper and hit him with it square on the nose in the middle of his report. Without flinching, he picked up the wad and threw it back at me, making a wisecrack under his breath. On the newscast the next morning, the paper wad incident aired just as it happened. Each year a party was held to show the comedy highlights from the newscasts, something unique in the news-reporting business.

Ted Turner encouraged this mockery of a news production because he claimed to hate the news. News was bad, nothing but gore and sensational violence, and Ted thought it was a bad influence on youthful viewers. His 3:00 a.m. presentation was his way of striking back. I suspected he just didn't have the money to put into the kind of news that would compete with the three major Atlanta channels and didn't want to pour money into something that would be so noticeably inferior. Without real news, he offered alternative, light-hearted, sometimes even mindless programming.

As we ended the 1975 season, Channel 17 seemed to be just one of the problems of the Braves. The team wasn't just awful; it was dull, and nobody in Atlanta seemed to be paying attention anyway. We scheduled an exhibition game between the Braves and Milwaukee Brewers, figuring that Hank Aaron's return would give us a big crowd to boost our spirits. We cancelled the game a week ahead of time when only two hundred tickets had been sold.

At the same time, however, I'd found in the three years since I'd met him that I really liked Ted Turner. Even with all his eccentricities, he was reliable when we needed something and a lot of fun to be around. We didn't see much of him but worked with his TV-station people regularly. They were good, professional people and did a fine job of televising the games. But we couldn't overlook our problems. The team was losing and attendance was last in the league.

And really, it had to be more than coincidence that the Braves had not been able to draw fans since the games started appearing so frequently on WTCG. More than a hundred games were now televised, many of them home games. The image and quality of WTCG were improving, but it was impossible not to wonder how all that TV exposure might be adding to our problems.

With too many baseball games for free on TV, would things ever be exciting again?

9

A NEW CAPTAIN
FOR THE TEAM

Each year during the first week of December all baseball executives gather for the traditional winter meetings. In 1972, for the first time, the winter meetings were held in Hawaii. The general managers set an all-time record for players traded in a week. They went to luaus, sat by pools, drank fruit drinks, and traded ballplayers at a frantic pace. Immediately following the winter meetings that year, it was announced that baseball would never go back to a sunny resort again. It was too much of a boondoggle, too much fun, and cost too much money. But in 1975, we were back on the beach in sunny Hollywood, Florida.

Rumors had been flying about the Braves. After such a miserable year at the gate, the baseball experts were beginning to question whether the South was the right place for a big-league club after all. Also, it was known that the Atlanta/LaSalle Corporation, which owned the Braves, was having trouble with some of its other companies and couldn't afford to keep a losing baseball team going. Something had to be done. The loudest rumor was that the Braves would be sold and moved to Toronto. That seemed far-fetched to me. The other rumor was that Ted Turner was about to buy the team. That one scared me to death. I had grown to like Ted but wasn't sure I was prepared to work for him.

Like remembering where I was when I heard JFK was shot or when the first man walked on the moon, I can remember the precise moment I heard that Ted Turner might buy the Braves. It was that kind of shock. I was walking down a staircase in the hotel lobby when a sportswriter approached me and asked me if what he had heard was true. I asked Bill Bartholomay and Dan Donahue to deny it. When they wouldn't say yes or no, I knew what the answer would eventually be.

Over the next few weeks the Braves started firing people who had been with the team for years. John Riddle, the long-time ticket director, was let go. John always had a dozen schemes working, and he was constantly in trouble with Charles Sanders, the business manager, over everything from expense accounts to ticket deals. But no one ever thought he'd get fired.

Dick Cecil, who had for years been the Braves' only vice president and had been the pivotal man in orchestrating the Braves' move to Atlanta, had resigned earlier in the year in what was said to be a power struggle between him and general manager Eddie Robinson. Since Eddie and Dick had totally different jobs, it now looked to us suspiciously like part of the trimming back in preparation for a sale.

Milo Hamilton, who had been the number-one radio and television announcer for the Braves since the move to Atlanta, was released from his contract and signed with the Pittsburgh Pirates. Ernie Johnson was moving to the top broadcast spot and would be joined by a young announcer from the minor leagues named Pete Van Wieren and by a Turner Broadcasting voice, Skip Caray, son of famous Chicago broadcaster Harry Caray.

I'd been quite vocal during the team's struggles. When the Atlanta newspaper was writing a story at mid-season about our attendance woes, they ran a picture of me sitting in the stands by myself with a pennant. The headline read, "Braves' Bob Hope Isn't Joking: Winning Sells."

The story by executive sports editor Lewis Grizzard read:

Bob Hope of the Atlanta Braves called the sports department the other day but not for the usual reason of offering information on the local major-league baseball team. 'I just wanted to hear a friendly voice,' he said.

'Dial-a-Prayer was busy.' It's been that kind of a year. When a sports publicity man starts counting on sportswriters for friendly words, it's obvious absolutely nothing is going right in life.

Bob Hope, director of public relations for the Braves, could have an easier job. He could have the Lester Maddox ax-handle concession at the Black Panther convention.

Instead, he must earn his daily bread selling the Braves to a populace already so hostile it seems ready to storm the stadium to burn it in protest—if anybody would go near the place.

Hope would probably even promote a 'Burn-the-Stadium Night' to draw a crowd if he weren't positive it would rain and douse the evening's festivities.

Basically, it has been his job to sell the ball club. Make people like the Atlanta Braves. Make them speak of the team in kind terms. Conjure inducements to lure people inside the stadium. Make them buy tickets.

The story continued, but by now it was obvious to everyone what single person should catch the blame for poor attendance. People weren't coming to games, and getting them to come was my job.

We were used to seeing players and managers come and go, but now the firings were spreading to the front office. So far I had been given more responsibility with each departure. But as author Robert Fields wrote in his biography of Ted Turner, if the Braves were sold, "most fans thought Bob Hope would be among the first to go." I was scared.

If I went, I was going to go down swinging. During the season I sent Mr. Donahue a memo telling him the only way we would get more excitement going for the team would be to have a strong local leader, someone who would act like a minor-league general manager and be out in the stands with the fans, be the number-one fan in town. We needed someone who would speak loud and clear and often about how great it is to have a team and how we would win someday. I had no suggestion as to who that person might be. But we needed a strong, visible leader.

At the end of the 1975 season, Frank Hyland of the *Atlanta Journal* interviewed me on what I'd do if I had a completely free hand promoting the Braves. I told him I thought we should make the stadium multicolored, install a giant television-like scoreboard, have promotions every night, fix up the concession stands to serve all kinds of food and have the most beautiful usherettes in baseball. I'd build picnic areas down the first and third baselines and paint the field in a rainbow of colors. It was a promoter's approach to baseball. He wrote the story. What he didn't write was what both Frank and I knew. Our team wasn't owned by promoters, but by very serious businessmen. One reason it was no longer fun to go to the ballpark was that our owners looked at baseball as a "serious" business. We needed someone who wanted it to be fun.

On January 6, 1976 — a month after I first heard the rumor in Hawaii — Dan Donahue phoned and asked me to come to his office. When I arrived, Phyllis Collins, his secretary, was sitting at her desk shaking her head dejectedly. She gave me a press release to read and told me to sit and wait for a moment. Mr. Donahue was in his office with the door closed. The press release was on Turner Communications Corporation letterhead with a notation to the media to call me if they needed more information.

"ATLANTA BRAVES SOLD TO TURNER COMMUNICATIONS" was the headline.

"The sale of the Atlanta Braves by parent company Atlanta/

LaSalle Corporation to Turner Communications Corporation was confirmed today in a joint announcement. The owners of the National League baseball team reached an agreement in principle to sell the Braves to an Atlanta-based broadcast group headed by R. E. "Ted" Turner, board chairman."

Ted Turner was now my boss.

When the door opened to Mr. Donahue's office, he and Ted Turner were sitting in there together. Mr. Donahue simply gave me a copy of the press release and asked me to get it to the media. Ted said he would be available to talk to anyone who wanted to interview him. In truth, Atlantans still had never heard of Ted Turner, and the news coverage of the sale the next day made it clear that even media people knew very little about the man who now owned the city's only professional sports team.

Turner called the next day and asked me to come to his television station and bring a baseball cap, a bat, and a script for him to read to make a TV commercial pitching season tickets. He was going to tape a television ad, and he would be the star.

I wrote a "Hi, I'm Ted Turner and I want you to buy Braves season tickets" script and showed up at his office the next day at four-thirty. When I got there, he was visiting with Spurgeon Richardson, the marketing director of Six Flags Over Georgia. My first thought was that Ted was trying to hire him for my job. I was ready to get fired right then.

Ted grabbed me when I walked in the door, marched down to the TV studio, and yelled for the cameras to start rolling. He put the cap on his head, threw the bat over his shoulder, and quickly read the script I had written. "Got it," he said. "I'll say it in my own words." He jumped in front of the camera, the lights went on and he started talking.

It was typical Ted Turner—going straight to Atlantans on television to ask them to buy tickets for his Braves. After a rousing spiel about tickets, Turner finished the commercial with "Call me when you need anything from the Braves, or if you can't reach me, call my pal Bob Hope at the stadium." Ted then told me to buy television advertising to run the spot on all three major Atlanta television stations over the next two weeks. I breathed a sigh of relief. Either my job was safe for at least a couple of weeks, or else he'd have to change the commercial. If he was telling people to call me, I thought I must be part of his plans.

The next day, Ted was having lunch with writer Wayne Minshew of the *Atlanta Constitution*. Minshew was a former minor-league pitcher, and, unlike other baseball beat writers who shifted to other sports every couple of years, he had been covering the team for the past fifteen seasons. Covering big-league baseball was his profession. Ted quickly grasped that Minshew could be just as good a source of information on the Braves for him as he could be for Minshew. The writer knew everything that had gone on with the team since its arrival in Atlanta and wasn't biased by having worked for it, so Turner used him over the next few months as one of his chief advisors. Ted's big scoop for Minshew that day was that he was considering changing the name of the team from the Braves to the Eagles, after his favorite racing sailboat, the American Eagle. Ted had bought the American Eagle after it had been humiliated in the America's Cup trials. He then worked on it, refitted it, and went on to an impressive series of victories in the Southern Ocean Racing Conference. That kind of turnaround was exactly what he intended for the Braves. He added that Eagles were cheaper to feed than Indians. And if the Braves didn't start winning, he said, he might change the name to the Turkeys.

The next day the headlines read, "Turner May Change Name of Braves to Eagles." The baseball world was outraged. Turner seemed shocked that such a seemingly minor consideration became such big news, but he also began to realize what kind of forum for national publicity he now had as owner of a major-league team. Virtually anything he said or did would be news. He could be a star. For the next couple of weeks, he went around singing a country song called "Rhinestone Cowboy" about "receiving cards and letters from people

I don't even know." Ted was loving the limelight.

Ted invited me to lunch the next week to talk about promotions. "Hope, I want this team to be like McDonald's. I want an atmosphere built here that will make kids want to come to the games. I want it to be exciting. Excitement isn't the success of one individual promotion, it's the chemistry of everything combined. We've got to do enough stuff to create that chemistry."

He asked me what we had on the promotion schedule. I told him. "That's not enough," he responded. I then told him all the ideas I'd sent to Dan Donahue in the past. We talked about the need for the fans to relate to the owner, to feel that the owner was a fan, a fan who sets the example by showing up every night at the games. The idea wasn't new to him. It was the approach he planned to take. On the spot, he approved every promotion I suggested and everything else I wanted to do, from building picnic areas along the baselines to painting the stadium seats in bright colors. When I'd suggest a promotion idea he particularly liked, such as Halter Top Night, he'd yell, "Aw right!"

Ted told me he wanted to be famous and that I could help. He wanted to be the "most famous man on earth next to Muhammad Ali." His plan was to use the Braves to help make himself a celebrity. He didn't care what kind of publicity he got. It was the basic lesson of journalism school. "Dog bites man" is not news. "Man bites dog" is news. He'd do whatever strange things it took to generate news and become famous. Once famous, he'd start worrying about what people thought of him.

I told him an old saying I'd heard from a South Carolina businessman: "It's better to be noticed as the village idiot than not to be noticed at all." He yelled "Aw right!" again. He was ready to become the "village idiot" if that was what it took to make him famous.

He told me the team probably wouldn't be very good at first, but he wanted me to "keep the smoke going after the fire goes out" with our promotions. We'd have so much action that no one would notice we weren't any good. All this sounded great to me. I was pleased and excited that he wanted me to be the catalyst for the chemistry he wanted to create. The guy was definitely a nut, but we were two peas in a pod.

The next day *People* magazine called. They wanted a photo of Ted standing in a rowboat in a pond wearing a Braves cap and holding a portable TV, a symbolic portrait of the three primary aspects of his new life—sailing, the Braves, and TV. The weather in January was bitter cold, but in his quest for fame he was more than willing.

Over the next few weeks Ted charged like a bull into the community that had not even known him before, relishing every opportunity to put himself in the spotlight. Before, people may have thought he was crazy, but fame legitimizes craziness and calls it eccentricity. Ted was now the colorful owner of the Atlanta Braves.

When asked at a Chamber of Commerce breakfast what he was going to do about the crime problems in the stadium parking lot, he said he would run buses from the stadium to the north side of town during games, let the thieves steal from the more affluent neighorhoods, then get them back on the buses and head back home after the games. That way the stadium would be safe.

He spoke at the Braves' Boosters Club annual banquet, giving a thousand of Atlanta's most avid baseball fans their first chance to see him. He told them he had Mafia friends in the North and would resort to roughing up other players around the league if necessary to win. He said he was serious about winning; the Braves slogan for the year would be "Victory or Death." He took a break during his speech to ask why the candles on the right side of the podium were burning faster than the ones on the left side. No one had noticed, but it was an interesting, if unrelated, point. The crowd was bewildered. No one knew what to think of the new team owner.

10

GETTING IN TOUCH WITH THE TEAM

Ted moved into his office at the stadium and was there every day hard at work. The pace was furious. He hosted a meeting of all the employees and talked for an hour. No one was quite sure what he meant, but they were all entertained and intrigued by what he said.

He changed our starting time for work from nine to eight-thirty so we'd get a half-hour head start each day on all the other teams in the league. He told us the Braves weren't as bad as the Polish air force in World War II. It could never even get its planes off the ground. He obliquely compared himself to Hitler and Alexander the Great and their conquests to take over the world. He said his college president told him the first day of school that in ten years he'd only remember the top three and the bottom three percent of the class. Ted knew he wasn't smart enough to finish on top, so he decided to finish on the bottom. He even started in on the environment, decreeing that anyone caught drinking from a styrofoam cup would be fired. He finished his speech to the office staff with what seemed to be a comfortable assurance he had straightened everything out.

As Ted's fame in the community grew over the next couple of weeks, so did mine. His TV spot telling everyone to "call Bob Hope" if they needed anything produced an endless backlog of calls, ranging from fans who wanted to try out for the team to a clothing store that wanted Ted to pose for its newspaper ads.

I referred the aspiring players to our farm department but asked Ted if he wanted to appear in the ads. After the Atlanta/ LaSalle owners, who were considered carpetbaggers from Chicago by most Braves fans, it was nice to have an owner that local companies wanted to showcase. Ted agreed to appear in the clothes ad, and we set up a date to take the pictures at the stadium.

When the day came for the photo shoot, Ted dressed in the new clothing and went down into the stadium seating next to the field to pose. After Ted had posed and changed shirts for an hour or so, the photographer left. Ted asked me to wait a few minutes for him. This was the first time he had been on the field with the bases in place, and he just had to circle them a couple of times. He completed the trip by sliding into home plate. Ted may have been the boss, but he was like a kid when it came to dealing with the ballplayers. They were his heroes.

Each January all the Braves players came to Atlanta for the annual team promotional caravan that toured southern cities. The first stop in 1976 was Ted's house for a party, his first chance to meet these special new employees that he admired so much.

Ted's home was nice, but modest. It certainly wasn't the kind of mansion that players might expect for a new team owner. All of the players arrived for cocktails before dinner, meeting Ted's wife Janie and the four of his five children who were still at home — Teddy, Beau, Rhett, and Jenny. Also there was Jimmy Brown, a black man who had taken care of Ted as a child and now took care of Ted's kids.

After dinner, the group gathered for the primary entertainment of the night. A projector and home-movie screen were set up in the living room, and a large reel was put on the projector. Ted told the group he was going to show them a movie to prove that he was an athlete, too, a movie about the

1974 America's Cup trials. He would show them his great attempt to capture the America's Cup. The attempt failed, he said, but he was certain the movie would impress them.

Ted nervously fidgeted with the projector and reel, threading the film quickly and turning it on. The film flickered, and he stopped it several times in an effort to get it on track. When he couldn't stop it from flickering, he just let it run, telling the players to just listen to the narration. Then the film broke. You could see Ted was crushed at having missed his first chance to impress the big-leaguers.

Ted had never been a baseball fan. In fact, before he bought the Braves, I had seen him only once or twice at games, and that was when the TV station was hosting its advertisers. Peter Dames, Ted's former school roommate, best friend, and president of Turner Outdoor Advertising, told me one night at the bar in the Stadium Club, "Hope, you and I are the only ones who realize Turner really hates going to these games."

But the big-league baseball players were his first exposure to professional athletes. They were famous and Turner seemed determined to impress them. He went to uncommon lengths to show that he was one of the guys. He started chewing tobacco and spitting in a paper cup, a practice virtually nonexistent outside the baseball world. He not only had his own locker in the team clubhouse; he would join the team in the showers.

His infatuation with the players put him at a distinct disadvantage in negotiating player contracts. The players knew they could get what they wanted as long as they negotiated directly with Ted. In general, Ted believed in giving people a little more than they expected to keep them happy.

Ted's negotiating prowess was seen at its best the time Rick Camp came in to talk contract. After having been out of the league the previous season, Camp had come back to lead the Braves' staff with twenty-two saves. Rick wanted $100,000 for the next season, and he wasn't going to settle for less. He went into Ted's office and announced, "I have a figure in mind and won't go below it."

Ted reportedly snapped back, "You don't tell me what you want. I own this team. I tell you what you get paid. You get a million dollars over three years, not a penny more." Actually, Camp earned most of it the next year when he set an all-time season record for relief pitchers by winning nine games, to go along with seventeen saves.

Ted was always inviting players to places where he thought he could impress them. On his second attempt to wow them with his sailing accomplishments, he took them as a group to the New York Yacht Club for dinner. He even sent a memo ahead of time to emphasize they had to wear coats and ties. This would be a nice place. The entire Braves team marched down the street behind Ted and right into the door of the club. Ted began by showing them some of the history of the place, telling about the model boats and trophies on display.

Then the team went into a private room for a prime rib dinner. This was Ted's most impressive moment with the team to this point in his baseball career. Suddenly his ears perked up. He heard something. Shortstop Darrel Chaney had invented a gadget out of a coathanger, a rubber band, and a washer. The rubber band held the washer stretched between a six- to eight-inch piece of the hanger. He would twist the washer tight, then sit on the contraption. Then, when he eased his weight off the thing, the washer would unravel and make a sound like someone letting gas. Ted heard the sound, then heard it again and again as the players passed the gadget around. Ted grew perplexed and uncomfortable. "What's wrong with you guys? You sick or something?"

Then the gadget was passed to Eddie Robinson, the stately general manager who was in his fifties. Eddie wound it up and took his turn. "Oh, no, not you too, Eddie!" Ted said in disgust. So much for trying to impress the players with the exclusive New York Yacht Club.

Ted did, however, take the team to Newport when he appeared in the America's Cup, and he regularly invited them to go to the places he enjoyed. He would take them to his Hope Plantation outside Charleston, South Carolina—five

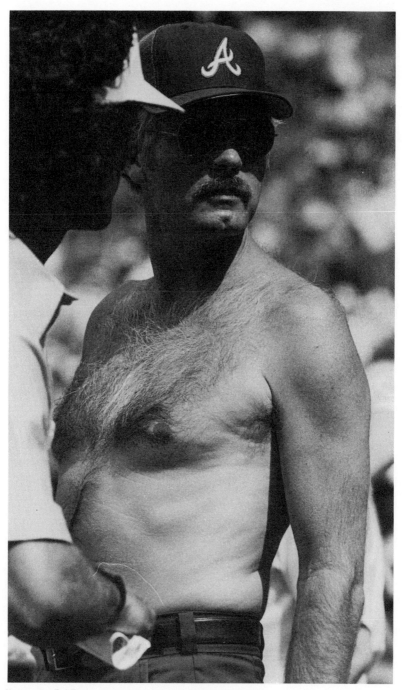

New owner Ted Turner proves he's a regular guy at the ballpark.

thousand acres of woods and wildlife — and they'd always come back with the same story of dodging Ted's gun barrel as he frenetically moved through the woods looking for game. Whenever Ted would turn to talk to someone, he would swing his rifle around and point it right at the person. The players were happy to get back alive.

Though many of Ted's efforts may have seemed misguided, they still made him a friend to most players. He quickly made it clear that they call him Ted or Turner, not Mr. Turner. Mr. Bartholomay and Mr. Donahue were the former owners. He was their pal, Ted.

While the players were accustomed to owners who were impeccably dressed at games, Turner wore a Braves cap and went without a shirt for day games. When he did dress up a little, the tie was likely a souvenir someone had given him, like his maroon "Hank Aaron 715" tie with Hank's picture all over it, and he wore a particular burgundy sport coat so often it seemed like he didn't own another one. Infielder Jerry Royster once approached him on the field before a game and jokingly asked, "Ted, have you ever noticed you look like you dress in a closet?"

Ted worked hard to seem down to earth, despite his yachting background, Ivy League education, and ownership of a TV station and big-league team. He drove an old Toyota and had his wife cut his hair at home. He worked hard to be ordinary, but really there was nothing ordinary about him.

11

TED'S FIRST SPRING TRAINING

Spring training is baseball's most frivolous tradition. It's held only at resorts, either in Florida, Arizona, or California. It starts in February, when the weather is cold in the North and everybody is looking for a reason to head for warmer climes. And it's training time for baseball, a game in which only the pitcher and catcher ever work up a sweat.

So spring training in baseball is virtually a boondoggle — a hundred guys getting together in a nice place, working out a little in the morning and then playing golf, fishing, or going to the beach in the afternoon. On top of that, the Braves' spring training camp is regarded as the most posh of all the elite sites to train — West Palm Beach, Florida, just across the bridge from elegant Palm Beach. As Harmon Killebrew put it once when his Minnesota Twins checked in to play an exhibition game against the Braves, "It's always nice to visit the Braves Country Club."

News was usually slow in spring training. Not much happened. The players just trained a couple of hours each day. But the media could always find a hot story. If not legitimate — like Aaron on the verge of breaking Ruth's record — then, well, illegitimate, like the year two Yankees pitchers swapped their wives and kids. It was treated on the sports pages like the biggest player trade of all time.

The spring training setting is laid back. Each team has a modest little stadium that seats six to ten thousand people, and in the Braves' case, trailers are set up on each side to serve as offices. Dress code is very casual. Shorts and T-shirt are office attire.

The players and their families look forward to Florida and spring training like a vacation. They generally rent a house and check the children out of their regular schools and into a local school in West Palm for a couple of months. As players practice each day, the wives and kids sit in the stands, and during breaks the players can walk over and talk. It's not exactly a picture of intensity.

Players' parents were always checking into spring training camps to see how their sons were doing. Dale Murphy was a young catcher for the team, and his father and mother were in town watching when he had a terrible streak of wildness while trying to throw out runners at second base. At a time when the Braves were trying to decide whether he should catch or play the outfield, Mr. Murphy told a reporter that "one thing certain is no one will steal centerfield on Dale." That quote swept through newspapers in spring training and, more than anything else, assured Dale's conversion to outfield.

Once when watching a Dodgers spring training game against the Braves, I sat behind a young Dodger player who was obviously in his first spring camp. I was entertained as he told his father the "inside story" on each of the players as they came to bat. "Phil Niekro—the players say his knuckleball jumps a foot," he said. "Tom Paciorek—the players think he'll be one of the best power hitters in the game," he noted. "Rowland Office"—referring to the Braves centerfielder— "Dad, the players say he's the ugliest man in baseball."

Susan and I would take our baby daughters Betsy and Clair to spring training, and we'd find players who'd babysit with them while we were out for dinner. Young Dale Murphy was one of our most reliable. He'd call Clair his "little buddy," and she'd call him "big buddy." Hall-of-Famer Luke Appling was in his seventies and still a Braves batting coach. He and his wife Faye also took care of the kids for us. In the afternoons, I'd take Betsy and Clair to the baseball field to fly a kite, and occasionally the players would have a fish fry at the field, cooking their catch of the past few days.

It was a setting made for Ted Turner. He could dock his boat nearby and sail each afternoon. He'd hang around the ballplayers morning and night. Also, it was an ideal setting for his free-spirited lifestyle. Ted was like the hyper child in a classroom. His nature was always to push the limit and see just how much he could get away with. And he could get away with virtually anything in spring training. There was no protocol—just show up for practice, wear whatever you want, talk to whomever you want whenever you want. Take it easy and have a good time. Easy orders. Ted was in his playpen.

Actually, his orientation to spring training in 1976 wasn't totally smooth. Major League Baseball conducted a lockout as part of its labor disagreement with players, and, as a result, Turner televised minor-league spring training games from Sarasota between members of the Braves' and the Chicago White Sox's farm teams. For a while, it looked like he'd never get his first big-league season underway.

But once Ted got into the swing of things, he took over the show. He learned all the players' lingo, like "not too shabby" for very good, or "bad" for good. He learned that "taters" and "dingers" were home runs and that "twirlers" and "hurlers" were pitchers. Calling a player "cool breeze" meant he was cool; calling a woman "cool breeze" meant she was hot. This was also the beginning of the "high-five" era, and the players had elaborate hand-shaking procedures that made every introduction a ritual. Spring training had a language all its own.

While most people moved at their leisure about the spring training camp, Ted looked like he was race-walking. You could sit in an office and watch him scoot back and forth in front of the window a half-dozen times every half-hour. He was always in a hurry for something, but it was hard to tell what, since not much happened in spring training. As Bill Lucas used to say, "Ted would make coffee nervous."

Ted's lifestyle was in full view of the world during spring training. There would be his French girlfriend, Frederique, for example — tall, dark-haired, big-eyed, glamorous, and exotic. Her beauty was highlighted by her clinging clothes and the fact that she obviously wore no underwear. She had reportedly been one of Ted's friends for years, even sailing as part of his crew. She lived in Paris but would show up at spring training, the World Series, and other special occasions. At the World Series one year, Ted left her in the hands of team broadcaster Pete Van Wieren, with my assistance if necessary. I told Pete to try to go it alone, and he took her to an ABC Television pre-game party and then sat with her during the game. I didn't go to the party but had a couple of dozen people ask about Pete and his friend that night. After the game at Yankee Stadium, I joined Pete and Frederique for the walk back to the car. Suddenly Pete and I turned to find that we had lost her. But she was already waiting at the car for us, having hitched a ride on the back of a horse behind one of New York's finest.

During spring training, Ted left town for a day and told the hotel manager to call either me or Pete if Frederique needed anything. I got the call first. Frederique was causing a problem. She was sunbathing in the nude by the pool, and she couldn't be talked into putting her clothes on. Pete and I jumped to the rescue, but, unfortunately, by the time we got there the problem had been solved. The crowd was still there, though, lingering on the balconies that surrounded the pool and forming a stadium for Frederique's show.

Ted's wife Janie also came to spring training, and although it was well known — even reported frequently in the media — that Ted had girlfriends, we still tried to be discreet in our conversations about the French "bombshell." Once a couple of us were talking about Frederique when Janie walked up. When we stopped too abruptly, she said, "You don't have to stop talking. I know who you're talking about, that French whore Ted hangs around with." So much for keeping any secrets from Janie.

Janie, a soft-spoken blonde in her late thirties, was Ted's second wife and mother of three of his children. She appeared to be a dedicated mother and stayed home with the kids while Ted traveled around the world pursuing his various interests. Janie was quiet and friendly, and all of us felt sorry for her because of the disrespect Ted showed. We were always prepared to help her out since Ted would routinely charge off after a game and leave her to find her own way home. Most of the time she was pleasant, even when her feelings were hurt. Occasionally she would cry. Janie showed the signs of living in the shadow of Ted's overpowering personality, and if she seemed to lack self-esteem, it was no wonder.

While in spring training one year, the Braves were contacted by CBS TV's "60 Minutes." They wanted to come spend a week with Ted. We were fairly skeptical since "60 Minutes" seldom did a puff piece on anyone and Ted was generally on his worst behavior in spring training. Ted's reputation as a wild man was already growing, and "60 Minutes" might have a field day with him.

Ted was unconcerned. He agreed to the "60 Minutes" interview, meaning a camera crew would follow him for a week everywhere he went. One of Ted's philosophies was that if you do outrageous things often enough, you're no longer outrageous, just colorful. He had a very colorful week with "60 Minutes."

On Thursday night, Ted hosted the Braves players and coaches for a team dinner. Ted was late and his entrance caused an earthquake. He came in with one of his lady friends at his side, and CBS cameras recorded the scene. Ted and Janie argued and Janie left crying. It looked like CBS had all it needed to do Ted in. Harry Reasoner was scheduled to fly in Sunday to interview Ted, wrapping up the crew's week of work.

I was told Reasoner was a big baseball fan and would enjoy his trip to spring training. We were scheduled to meet him in my office at West Palm Beach Municipal Stadium at one o'clock. The interview would take about two hours. Ted said he would be there and ready on time.

At about 12:30, Mr. Reasoner showed up. He was pleasant and happy to be in a spring-training camp, and he looked just like he did on television. We sat in the Braves' dugout and watched the workout while we waited for Ted. I was impressed how much he knew about baseball and enjoyed being with the players, several of whom sat around talking to him.

Once, while he was looking at infield practice, Mr. Reasoner asked about one of the infielders. "The second baseman looks older than the other players," he noticed. "Who is he?" I explained that it was Al Thornwell, owner of an Atlanta electrical supply company and member of the Braves' board of directors. Sometimes Braves owners and directors would show up and dress out with the team. Potter Palmer, whose family founded the Palmer House Hotel in Chicago, used to work out nearly all spring with the club. We used to say Potter's playpen was the lobby of the Palmer House when he was a baby and a big-league baseball stadium when he grew up. Al was just as avid as Potter, just a lot older.

I explained to Mr. Reasoner that while I was always worried about Al getting hurt playing with the professionals, the players took the opposite view. They had an on-going contest, their version of target practice. The name of the game was "Hit Al and Win." Whenever a player hit a ball that knocked Al down, the rest of the players had to pay him a quarter. About that time, Al was hit by a line drive and carried off the field. You would have thought the batter had won the lottery.

Mr. Reasoner said he was amazed a big-league team would allow someone to work out with them like that. I thought for a moment and was pretty amazed, too. But we'd always allowed it.

Thornwell, I explained to him, was a special case. Everybody figured he was Ted's spy in the clubhouse, checking every move the coaches and players made. In fact, they called him "Inspector Clouseau," partly because he looked like Peter Sellers and because he was always snooping around. Awarding money for hitting an old man with a baseball seemed unkind, but less so if he was a spy.

We had waited for Ted for more than an hour when Mr. Reasoner told me he was troubled by the interview he was about to do. "From everything I've read about Ted Turner and everything I've heard from our crew about him this week, I just don't like the man. I've never done an interview when I've gone into it with such a negative feeling about someone. I just don't like the guy."

I thought to myself, Ted is in for it now. And on top of that, he's already an hour late for the interview. Another hour passed and Ted still hadn't shown up, and the entire CBS crew was getting madder by the moment. "60 Minutes" was going to do us in. Eventually Ted came bounding around the corner and into the field.

"Mr. Reasoner," he said, "I am such a big fan of yours and I'm so sorry to be late. Let me explain. I was shopping with my wife and family. I get so little time with them. I didn't have the heart to leave. I brought them with me. Let me introduce you to my wife Janie, daughter Jenny, my sons Teddy, Rhett, and Beau.

"Where do you want me for the interview?" he continued, in his raspy but apologetic voice. "I know this is rude, but I need to get it over with in an hour. I've promised the boys I'd take them fishing this afternoon. I can't let business stand in the way of fishing with my sons. I don't have time to spend with them very often."

When Ted went out on the field for his "60 Minutes" interview, those of us in the dugout just shook our heads at each other. This, I still thought, could be the beginning of the end.

When the interview was over, Ted and his family left. Harry Reasoner walked back into the dugout and thanked me. "I had Ted all wrong," he said. "People just don't understand him. He's one of the most refreshing, delightful people I've ever met. A real American hero. He's just a maverick and marches to a different drummer."

Oh brother, I thought, Ted did it again. The segment aired and told the world what Ted wanted the world to know. Ted Turner was a hero. Just ask "60 Minutes."

12

THE NEW GAME OF TEDDYBALL

There are few things in life as fresh and exhilarating as the opening game of a baseball season. Regardless of how great or miserable the previous season might have been, the record is cleared and there's the chance that this new season can be "the year." In fact, opening night is the moment when the "next year" of "wait 'til next year" arrives.

Of course, opening night wasn't always so wonderful for the Braves. There were sensational ones, like the first in Atlanta in 1966 when major-league baseball officially arrived in the South. There was 1974 with Hank Aaron's home-run record. Both were sold out and were games that everyone on hand will always remember. Then there were the ones more easy to forget.

The Braves spent much of their time in the 1970s at the bottom of the league standings, and even with the fresh start of a new season, fans were hardly optimistic, much less excited. When Ted Turner purchased the team in 1976, the opening-night crowd the previous year had been a miserable 12,774 — the smallest in baseball.

Ted had his heart set on selling out his first opening night. He came close, drawing 37,973 fans. He even went down onto the field before the game and directed the crowd in singing "Take Me Out to the Ballgame."

Turner celebrates his first opening night by leading the crowd in "Take Me Out to the Ballgame."

Turner seemed totally committed to doing whatever was necessary to make the Braves a success. "I bought the Braves because I'm tired of seeing them kicked around, of seeing the headlines about Losersville. You can see it in the streets," he declared. "If the team's doing well the people walk with a little more pride."

On April 10, he signed Andy Messersmith, the thirty-year-old former Dodger pitcher who had won nineteen games the previous season and had two twenty-game winning seasons during his eight-year big-league career. The signing of Messersmith was not only evidence of Ted's commitment to winning but also proof that top-quality players believed Ted could build the Braves into a winner. Messersmith had several big offers and could have gone to a number of winning teams. But he was obviously convinced the Braves were on the right road. His becoming a Brave was also a vote of confidence for Ted from the Braves team. Four players who had been with the Dodgers the previous year — Jimmy Wynn, Tom Paciorek, Jerry Royster, and Lee Lacey — had spent the winter and spring as Braves and told their friend Messersmith that Atlanta was the right place to come. It looked like good things were ahead.

My challenge from Ted to promote his new team with all my might saw its first results on Easter, the first Sunday game of the season. Easter had always been a terrible day to play baseball in Atlanta, an impossible day to draw a crowd. We decided to make it a special day for the youngsters by spreading Easter eggs all over the field after the game and allowing all youngsters down on the field for the world's largest Easter-egg hunt. The idea was a perfect mesh with Ted's desire to make the stadium a family place. Since the crowd would be small, the number of kids would be small. Yet they'd have the chance to run around on the big-league field, go back to school and tell all the other kids what a good time it was, and then more would start coming to the games. Easter eggs are also cheap. So the promotion wouldn't cost us much in case it got rained out or no kids wanted to participate. It seemed like a reasonable event to launch our new promotional strategy.

Easter turned out to be a bigger day than I could have imagined. Manager Dave Bristol announced it would be the first start for Messersmith. Suddenly ticket sales started taking off, and a crowd we projected at ten thousand jumped to well over forty thousand. To prepare, I sent my new group sales manager, Kris Krebs, out to buy more eggs.

The Easter-egg hunt was Krebs's first big project since joining the Braves during the winter. He was a former shortstop in the Boston Red Sox and Washington Senators minor-league system and also a native of Atlanta. He loved baseball and was thrilled to be involved with the team. He had been an insurance salesman when I hired him, and he said he was willing to do anything for the Braves. The Easter-egg hunt was his chance to prove it.

The logistics of the egg hunt were basic. Kris bought several thousand foil-wrapped chocolate eggs and another few thousand colored candy ones. The eggs filled several dozen large cardboard boxes stored in our offices a couple of days prior to the big event. Mixed in with the chocolate and candy eggs were plastic ones with little slips of paper inside. The paper slips could be redeemed for assorted prizes like Braves caps, T-shirts, game tickets, and even some toys Kris persuaded a local toy store to donate. Right after the game ended, Kris would take several members of the stadium ground crew to our offices to get the boxes of eggs. They would then spread the eggs all over the field for the youngsters to find. What could be simpler?

However, the growing size of the crowd was a concern. Not only did we purchase more eggs, but we also beefed up the number of ushers who would be in the stands and on the field to help the smaller children. We weren't sure how many youngsters might participate in the hunt, but estimates were fairly easy to make. We knew that for a Bat Day—the biggest draw of all kids promotions at the stadium—about a third of the crowd would be twelve or under. We figured that few kids older than six or seven would want to participate in an egg hunt, so that would cut the number of participants to about a sixth of the crowd. Since the event would be after the game and only half the crowd ever sticks around for a post-game activity, that would cut the number in half again. Basically we were talking about a couple of thousand kids. Max.

Andy Messersmith's debut as a Brave was over in a hurry. He had missed all of spring training while negotiating his contract, and rather than spend a few weeks throwing in preparation for his first start, he and manager Bristol decided to put him under the fire of a real game. He had stayed in shape during the spring, and Bristol took a five-mile jog with him from Atlanta Stadium to the Grant Park Zoo and back. Messersmith didn't even break a sweat and told Bristol he was ready to play. Bristol thought it was worth a shot.

Messersmith may have been in shape, but his arm wasn't. He was knocked out of the game early. From Kris's and my viewpoint, that was good news. Since the new pitcher was the person the crowd showed up to see, we thought most of the crowd would leave early. We were convinced we had everything well in hand. But in looking through the stands, a crowd of forty thousand looks a little ominous when you're about to invite them down on the field after the game.

When the game ended, Krebs and his crew of assistants headed for the office to get the boxes of eggs. In the meantime, new Braves radio announcer Pete Van Wieren had volunteered to do the honors of emceeing the hunt from a microphone set up on the field behind home plate. Pete would instruct the youngsters to walk down the steps located at the six gates leading from the stands to the field. They would be told to line up along the first and third baselines and await the start of the hunt. Easy enough.

Pete took his place behind the mike at home plate. The youngsters were in the stands, lined up and pressing forward to the gates, ready to come down on the field at Pete's instruction. We waited, but the eggs weren't showing up. One of the ground-crew assistants ran up to me and said they were locked out of the offices. They needed a key. I gave him my key and we waited another ten minutes until a dozen ground-crew helpers and a smiling, waving Kris Krebs walked from the right field gate onto the outfield grass, each with a big box of eggs. I was getting anxious during the long wait, but now things seemed to be going smoothly. The ground crew started spreading the eggs across the field, and Pete announced for the youngsters to start coming down the steps to line up for the start.

Suddenly the dam broke. A swarm of youngsters — thousands — jumped the stadium railing and stampeded past Pete, heading for the outfield eggs. It looked like a buffalo herd in an old cowboy movie. Pete was trying vainly to tell them to line up along the baselines, but the swarm was racing right by him. The ground crew, struck with fear, dropped their boxes of eggs and ran to escape by jumping the outfield fence. Within seconds, all eggs were gone.

Pete pleaded into the microphone and was able to bring

some order to the chaos and get the kids back behind the lines. Kris came over and reported that only about half the eggs were gone. They hadn't been able to bring all the boxes out on the field. The rest were in the stadium tunnel. Pete and I decided that, after the initial shock, we now had things in order. The crowd of kids, though staggeringly large, was standing in order waiting for further instructions. Kris and his crew were sent for the rest of the eggs.

While waiting, Pete and I perused the stadium stands. It didn't seem like there were nearly enough adults for all the children. We never have understood it. Out of a crowd of forty thousand, it looked like most of them were six years old and standing on the field.

Kris and the ground crew now had their boxes in hand and were marching back across the outfield grass. This time Kris wasn't smiling. Pete started to make the announcement for the kids to line up and get ready, but the chaos broke loose again. This time Kris had told the guys to hold on to the boxes and not panic, to make sure they threw all the eggs out on the field. The scene was like an Alfred Hitchcock movie — children swarming like birds after adults who were running for their lives, throwing eggs in the air. After emptying their boxes, the ground-crew members fled to the nearest safe spot. Some jumped the outfield fence again. One climbed a potted tree in the first-base picnic area, crouching in the top as a mob of kids at the base stretched tiny arms for one more egg.

So the first big promotion of the year had been not just a flop but a disaster. The only salvation was that no one got seriously hurt. Someone could have been killed. Also, it was fortunate that Ted had left the game early. If he had stayed, I was certain I'd have been out of job.

The next morning the Braves' executive staff sat around the conference table at nine o'clock waiting for Ted to arrive. My fear of this meeting had kept me awake all night. My only hope, I thought, was if somehow Ted hadn't heard about the eggs. Then Ted walked in the room and looked right at me. "Hope, heard the Easter-egg hunt got a little out of hand," he said. "Don't let it slow you up. Keep up the good work."

The Easter-egg hunt may have gotten out of hand, but it really wasn't all that strange when compared to some of the things baseball teams have done as promotions in the past. The term "baseball promotion" conjures up an assortment of strange and not so sensible activities designed to encourage more people to attend games. Bill Veeck, the great flamboyant promoter for the St. Louis Browns and Chicago White Sox, contributed more than anyone else to the acceptability of almost any activity in the guise of a baseball promotion. From exploding scoreboards to a pinch-hitting midget, Veeck made the absurd seem reasonable.

Each team has its own distinct promotional philosophy. The Chicago Cubs, for instance, had a terrific and inexpensive approach. None. They just played baseball. They played only in the daytime, which made it inconvenient for most people to attend, and they had no special days at Wrigley Field, their rickety old ballpark. No Bat Days, no Old-Timers Days, no Photo Days, no nothing. Just plain baseball at the worst possible time in the worst possible place. It worked. The result was maniacal fans who jammed the stadium and were fiercely proud that they needed no promotions to entice them to support a team that hadn't won a pennant in nearly fifty years. It was like native New Yorkers bragging that their Big Apple is the greatest city in the world, while ignoring the crime, slime, and grime as it crumbles away.

Even the fans got into the Cubs' act. They formed the Bleacher Bums in the outfield seats, making the worst seats in the stadium the most coveted. But there's more. Other teams lost hundreds of baseballs each season when they were hit into the stands during the games. Fans kept the balls as souvenirs. But when a home run was caught in the stands by a Bleacher Bum, the bum was tradition-bound to throw it back onto the field.

In New York, even losing became a great promotion for the old Mets. The worst they got, the better it got for them. Fans would cheer as they'd turn the simplest catches into spine-tingling thrillers. Sadly, the 1969 Mets screwed up the whole deal by winning. They were World Champions, and losing would never be so much fun again.

Some teams built their promotions around tradition. The pinstripes of the Yankees were worn by players performing in the "House that Ruth Built" with plaques to Ruth, Gerhig, Mantle, DiMaggio, and other immortals lining the outfield wall. In Los Angeles, the Dodgers organization was always talking about "bleeding blue," and their own winning tradition, their clean stadium, and their penchant for doing things first class amounted to all the promotion they needed.

But for most other clubs, promotion meant hard work, getting out there and scrambling for ticket sales any way they could. That's the way it was for the Braves, and Ted was determined to scramble harder than anyone.

The power to promote is potentially dangerous. A big-league team's promoter has strange and exotic powers at his control. He is capable of telling people to do ridiculous things and having them actually do those things. The teams play in stadiums that have public address systems and giant lighted message boards, so the team can tell everyone at the games anything. The teams also have radio and television networks to broadcast the games, and they can use those broadcasts to tell people what they want them to do. Then there's the advertising the team runs in newspapers, the newsletters they send out to fans, and even the publicity from the constant media coverage. If anyone wanted to take advantage of this access to baseball fans, he certainly could.

I found out early in my career about a baseball team's awesome ability to make fans do things. We had a message-board operator, Red Mullins, who would sit at an electronic typewriter and type the messages that would then appear on the lighted centerfield board. Each message could contain up to six lines of forty-eight characters, ample space for most instructions to the fans. There was no such thing as computer storage back then. Red would type what he wanted to appear, and it was recorded on a long strip of pink-paper tape. The pattern of holes in the tape could be read by a machine and converted to the desired message on the board. Red would write a code on each tape that would signify to him what message it contained. Sometimes Red would get the tapes mixed up.

The lighted message board was huge and located on the ground level directly behind the left-centerfield fence. When a message appeared, no one could miss it.

One game, in the middle of the sixth inning, Red put in a tape to generate a message. I don't know what the message was supposed to be, but what appeared were instructions for the crowd to stand and sing the national anthem. So right in the middle of the sixth, the game stopped, the crowd rose to its feet and started singing, and even the players and umpires joined in. Amazing.

I had all this power at my fingertips, and I was willing to use it. Once, for instance, we were going to serve fans watermelon on the field after a game. We wanted to make the event more special and decided to have a frog-jumping contest, like the one Tom Sawyer held. Only problem, we didn't know where to find frogs. Easy solution! We made our plea on the public-address system, on the message board, on television and radio. We needed frogs for a frog-jumping contest. It was "bring your own frogs." Thousands of frogs were on hand that day for the game. People had gone deep into the swamps of south Georgia and brought frogs to the stadium in picnic coolers. We had our frog-jumping contest. And frogs were croaking underneath the stadium for months.

I was certain now that the combined effort of Hope and Turner might test the limit. We were intent on using promotions to keep the body kicking even if the team was dead. And dead it was. After starting the 1976 season with an 8-5 record to lead the division, the Braves lost thirteen games in a row, the most for any team since 1906. It was last place for the rest of the way. In fact, it would be last place for the next 635 games.

Our promotional strategy was simple. It had two elements.

We intended to have as many promotions as humanly possible. We also intended to give as many fans a chance to actually walk on the big-league field before and after games as possible. We figured the combination of the two would keep the action high and the people happy. After all, if one promotion is good, two must be better and hundreds would be close to heaven. Also, how could anyone who actually touches a foot on a big-league playing field not become a fan for life?

We gave fans plenty of opportunities to walk on the big-league field. Hundreds of thousands of little-leaguers, cheerleaders, town mayors, band members, choruses, dancers, honorary bat boys, home-run contest participants, first-ball throwers, and national-anthem singers would march around the field before the games.

We started honoring one community each game as the official Community Night in a pre-game ceremony. The mayor would get a plaque, someone from the town would sing the anthem, someone else would throw out the first ball. Eventually we were honoring several communities every game, giving out plaques to dozens of mayors, and more people were participating in the first-ball ceremony than playing in the game.

If someone wanted to sing the national anthem, we let them stand right there on the field and do it, no questions asked. Most were fine, a few were awful, and only once did we turn anybody down. A coed from Auburn University wanted to play it on a saw. We made her audition and she was great. She played the saw like a violin, and it was amazing how good it sounded. But even if it sounded fine, it seemed just a little too disrespectful, even for us.

Ted Turner was not only a supporter of the promotions but frequently a participant—either as planned or spontaneously. When outfielder Ken Henderson hit his first home run in Atlanta, Ted jumped the railing next to the dugout and ran out to home plate to congratulate him. No owner had ever run on a big-league field during a game to congratulate a player. Some baseball officials were outraged, feeling his action was

Susie the base-sweeper and her assistant, Betsy Hope.

beneath the dignity of the owner of a major-league club. Others thought the gesture showed good, clean enthusiasm and support for his team. Regardless, photos of Ted on the field shaking hands with Henderson were in papers across the nation. For Ted, it was more fame — but he was still just beginning.

At the end of the fifth inning, there's a short break in baseball when the ground crew runs out on the field with a screen to drag and smooth out the infield dirt. Most baseball teams followed the lead of the Baltimore Orioles, who came up with the idea of having a pretty girl in shorts and a team shirt run around the infield and sweep the bases. As with virtually everything we did, we decided to take the Orioles' concept to the extreme. When we'd take our fifth-inning break, our Susie Sweeper would take the field with her broom, joined by our big green fuzzy mascot, the Bleacher Creature, who would turn flips as Susie ran from base to base. They were often accompanied by a four-year-old girl in the same Braves outfit as Susie, also with a broom and carrying a Bleacher Creature stuffed animal under one arm. This little girl added a cute touch to the ceremony and was one of my favorites, since she was my daughter, Betsy.

The routine each game was for Betsy to stay with me in the press box, and the teenage girl playing the Susie Sweeper role would come get her during the fourth inning. The two of them would join the Bleacher Creature in the first-base dugout, ready to run on the field at the last out of the fifth inning. One night I looked for Betsy in the picnic area and saw Ted down there with her, along with Susie and the Creature. When the time came to run on the field, there was Ted right alongside them, running around the bases and turning somersaults. He was hardly your typical team owner.

The 1976 Olympics were taking place in Montreal, so we decided to have our own version of the Olympics between the Braves and Phillies before a game. We bought basketballs, footballs, peach baskets, barrels, hula hoops, and even tricycles to develop our own set of Olympic sports for the occasion.

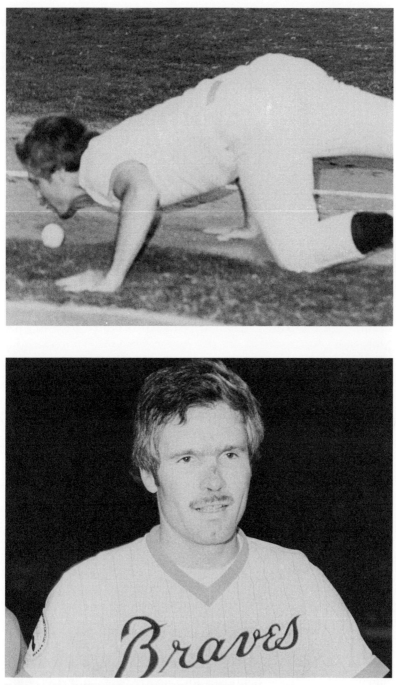

Turner was bloodied but victorious in the Baseball Nose Push.

The players joined right in, and the contests were heated. Throwing a basketball from home plate to hit in a barrel at second base is almost impossible. Few players hula-hoop well. Hitting a peach basket at ninety feet with a football is also tough. But the players were willing to participate in all the events, with one exception. No Brave wanted to do our version of an egg race — the Baseball Nose Push.

The event would be grueling. A Phillie would line up on his knees at first base; a Brave would get on his hands and knees at third. Both would have baseballs. The first one to push the baseball with his nose all the way to home plate would be the winner.

Several Braves attempted to push baseballs with their noses and quickly concluded they weren't the ones to compete. The only Phillie to volunteer was ace reliever Tug McGraw. We needed a Brave. I looked to Kris Krebs. "Where's Ted?" I asked. In a twinkling, Kris had Ted ready at third base to race McGraw.

One risk of trying new competitions is that undetermined factors can effect the outcome. In the Baseball Nose Push, there were several impediments. First, a baseball is very hard and can hurt your nose. The laces of the baseball make it difficult to roll and can hurt your nose even more. And finally, the dirt sticking to the ball, on top of the hard leather and the laces, can really hurt your nose.

When the starting gun sounded, the dust was flying furiously from both Ted and Tug. But neither was covering much distance. The way they were inching along, it looked like we might be in for a delayed start of the baseball game. Then, in a burst of energy, Ted started jamming his forehead into the ball and shoving it in the direction of home plate. His forehead and nose were looking like he had been flayed, but Ted reached home victorious. Tug was still near first, tentatively trying to roll the ball along. Ted, in his Braves uniform, rose to his feet the winner, smile on his face, blood from his hairline to the tip of his nose, and bloody baseball raised high in one of his hands. The crowd cheered.

Ted kept the blood-stained baseball on his desk the remainder of the season. He would point to it and tell people I was the only person in the world who could do that to a boss and get away with it. But mostly he used it as an excuse to brag about his great victory over Tug McGraw.

13

OF OSTRICH RACES AND OTHER MARVELS

One day I read an article — don't ask me where — about ostriches that could be rented for races. The article made clear that ostrich races generally took place at county fairs, but I realized they'd be perfect entertainment prior to a Braves game.

Frankly, I'd never seen an ostrich race, and it was strange indeed to imagine people climbing on the back of a huge bird and galloping away, but I could only assume that was the way it was done. I asked Ted if he would be willing to race local celebrities. He was.

An artist drew a cartoon of Ted sitting in a saddle racing on the back of an ostrich, and we used the drawing in the ads for the game. The Great Ostrich Race. Ted was to race against *Atlanta Journal* sportswriter Frank Hyland, one of the most willing participants in our promotions but also one of Ted's most bitter foes. When Ted fired Donald Davidson, Hyland wrote: "Ted Turner has money. Ted Turner has a lot of money. Ted Turner has enthusiasm. Ted Turner has his own baseball team. Ted Turner belongs to some of the world's most prestigious clubs. But Ted Turner has no class." Ted never forgot that story. There was no one he would rather defeat than Hyland, and an ostrich would be his weapon.

Also participating in the race would be Braves broadcasters

Skip Caray, Ernie Johnson, and Peter Van Wieren and a local Atlanta disc jockey, Skinny Bobby Harper. To bring the highest possible degree of credibility to the competition, I called Churchill Downs to get the name of a company that made racing silks and then had the company make official, brilliantly colored silks for all our jockeys. On the back were nicknames: Frank Hyland was "Poison Pen," Skip Caray was "Skippy Star," and Ernie Johnson was "Big E."

When the day of the event arrived, people were intrigued, if nothing else. Piercing questions arose, like "How do you guide the ostrich?" or "Will an ostrich be able to hold up under the weight of 250-pound Skip Caray?" or "Do ostriches bite?" It was a seminal event in the history of curiosity.

The morning of the race, groundskeeper Robert Johnson phoned to tell me a trailer of "turkeys and pigs" had arrived at the entrance of the stadium tunnel. I knew the "turkeys" had to be our ostriches; the "pigs" turned out to be camels that were thrown in for free with the ostrich rental.

The ostrich owner explained to me the procedure for the race. Actually, the riders weren't going to sit on the backs of the birds; they would sit in little carts that the ostriches pulled. The jockeys would not, as a matter of fact, be able to control the speed of the birds. Our ground crew would simply hold on to the animals until the start of the race and then let go. On the other hand, the riders would be able to steer—with a broom, no less. Place the broom where it blinds the field of vision of the right eye, and the bird goes left. Flip the broom to block the other eye, and it goes right. That's the way to drive an ostrich.

The day of the race *Sports Illustrated* writer Ron Fimrite was in Atlanta to do a story on Turner. Ted was frantic. He wanted everything about the race to be perfect and legitimate. Somehow, legitimacy hadn't been one of the things I had thought much about when organizing the event.

Ted, trying to impress Fimrite with his appreciation for the tradition of baseball, had said, "Some things don't need changing. The sunrise doesn't need changing, moonlight

The Great Ostrich Race—another first for baseball promotions.

doesn't need changing, azaleas don't need changing, and baseball doesn't need changing." Then Ted rushed out of the interview to race an ostrich before the game.

Ted brought Fimrite to my office for the pre-race briefing. I explained to Ted how he was to race the ostrich by riding in a cart behind it and guiding the bird with a broom. Ted was incensed. "We've told everyone I'm riding on the back of an ostrich. That's false advertising. I won't do it. Cancel the race!"

Ted said he feared the race would make a mockery of him, rather than present him as the serious business leader that he wanted people to respect him for being. He told me I was making people think he was crazy. It seemed a little late to worry about that. The fact that people weren't surprised to see him racing an ostrich makes it pretty clear what the public's attitude toward him was.

I felt totally ridiculous trying to convince someone to fulfill an obligation to race an ostrich, and especially trying to argue that the ostrich race would be legitimate. How legitimate can an ostrich race be? Finally, Ted conceded he would go through with it.

I gave Ted his green racing silks and his eyes lit up. Obviously, this official racing outfit would contribute to the "legitimacy" he was seeking. Then, as he looked at the back of his shirt, his face dropped. "Why 'Teddy Ballgame'?" he asked, looking at the nickname stitched on it. "Nobody calls me 'Teddy Ballgame.' That's disrespectful. My name is Ted."

The truth was that virtually everyone associated with the Braves was calling him "Teddy Ballgame" back then. The nickname originally was used for Ted Williams, but Ted's lighthearted and enthusiastic approach to team ownership seemed better suited for it. When the sportswriters would call up to check on the team, they'd ask, "Where's Teddy Ballgame today?" Or if I was rushing off to a meeting and someone asked where I was going, I'd say, "I'm having lunch with Teddy Ballgame." Nobody ever asked me who I meant. We all called him that, but apparently no one had called him Teddy Ballgame to his face.

Ted walked dejectedly out of my office with his racing silks in hand. A few minutes later I walked into his office and he was sitting at his desk with a razor blade and glue. He had cut every letter off the back of his shirt, and no longer was he "Teddy Ballgame." He had used the glue to replace it with a more respectful "Ted." His complex personality was in conflict with itself. He was about to do something to enhance his reputation, but his reputation was part and parcel of the wacky, maverick image he both loved and hated at the same time.

"You've made people think I'm crazy," he told me again. I just smiled and told him not to worry about it. There were worse things than being crazy, and at least we were having a good time.

By the time the actual race arrived, Ted was back in vigorous spirits. Six giant ostriches pulling six sulkies looked every bit as big league and important as an ostrich race can possibly look. The crowd cheered as the individual jockeys in their colorful uniforms were introduced. Each jockey nervously climbed in place as the ground crew fought to hold the huge birds that were obviously anxious to run.

The first heat would be between Skinny Bobby Harper and Pete Van Wieren. Then Skip Caray would take on Ernie Johnson. Finally, the featured race of the day would be Frank "Poison Pen" Hyland against Ted "Ted" Turner.

The jockeys received their broom-guidance instructions, and soon the first heat was off and running. Pete raced as if he had done it all his life, expertly navigating the route from the first-base dugout down the first-base foul line, around the outfield warning path, down the third-base foul line, past the visiting Dodgers' dugout and finishing behind home plate. Skinny Bobby's guidance system was out of whack. His ostrich raced toward the right-field tunnel gate, which was slammed shut just in time by the ground crew to keep the bird from pulling him out of the stadium into the parking lot and possibly onto I-75. Then the ostrich turned and headed straight into the Dodgers' dugout.

The next heat went much more smoothly. Ernie and Skip were in control, and both birds trotted briskly around the field. Ernie's ostrich pulled into the Dodgers' dugout for a quick pit-stop, but got back on track to finish the race. Skip's bird never let up and won going away.

The final and most important race was by far the most dramatic. Both Ted and his bird were nervous. The ostrich kept jerking and lurching ahead and the ground crew kept pulling it back behind the starting line. Ted dropped his broom while frantically trying to figure out how to use it. He nervously chewed on his tobacco and spit on the grass repeatedly. Hyland sat smiling, asking, "What have you gotten me into this time?" He seemed comfortable with his steering system.

When the gun was fired, Ted's bird took off, but not in the right direction. It sped across the outfield toward Chief Noc-A-Homa's teepee in left field, then turned and headed counter-race-wise along the outfield fence. Finally it turned and charged directly into the Dodgers' dugout, scattering players like feathers. In the meantime, Hyland's ostrich was slow starting but stayed on track. He guided it carefully around the path and passed Ted, who was still stuck in the dugout, on his way to victory.

It was a bitter defeat for Turner, possibly the most bitter since being humiliated in the America's Cup trials.

Ted's presence was obvious at all the games. He'd sit in his seat on the first row to the home-plate side of the Braves' dugout, and from there he'd conduct his business for the game. He'd talk to the players as they ran on and off the field, jump up and down cheering, and sign autographs or have his photo taken with fans. When the team started losing early in the year and was getting beat badly in a game, Turner rushed to the press box one night to announce to the crowd over the public address system: "This is a new policy for the time being. Nobody is going to leave here a loser tonight. I want you all to come back here tomorrow night as my guests. I'm in this for life, and we appreciate your support. We do. We're going to beat the hell out of these guys who're beating the hell out of us right now!"

Turner gave them all a free ticket to the next night's game, and what's more, he had a live microphone installed next to his seat in the stands so he could talk to the crowd whenever he wanted.

Some of the promotions we held during the year were baseball standards, like Bat Day, Cap Day, T-Shirt Day, the Old-Timers Game, Banner Day and Poster Day. But many had never been tried before and will probably never be tried again. One Friday-night game was declared Mattress-Stacking Night. It was combined with 25-cent Beer Night. College fraternities and sororities from all over the Southeast were invited to attend the game and bring their own mattresses. Following the game, we'd have a competition on the field to determine which group could win a spot in the Guinness Book of World Records by stacking the most people on top of a single double bed mattress in one minute. We had four referees in striped shirts and a time-keeper on the field ready to judge the sixteen fraternities and one sorority that registered for the competition.

Mattress stacking was a college fad that turned out to be fairly dangerous. The kids would pile on top of each other, crushing the ones on the bottom. With about two thousand college students on the field competing, Sigma Chi Fraternity of Emory University had a surprise participant. Ted joined their team. I watched as Ted jumped on the mattress at the bottom of the pile and turned red-faced as the others piled on top. His team didn't win.

"Why do you let me do these kinds of things?" he asked me afterwards. "I've got to stop. I'll kill myself and I've never even been to a World Series."

Our efforts to get everyone involved in the act never faltered. Skinny Bobby Harper was invited back to participate again when Baskin-Robbins wanted to have a promotion at the Stadium. We decided to have a "chilling leap into the world's largest dish of ice cream." Harper was the dare-devil and promoted the event on his morning radio show on WGST. Kris Krebs, of course, was the man assigned to assemble the dish of ice cream.

Baskin-Robbins donated their "seconds," the ice cream that wasn't good enough for them to sell, and Kris spent the day of the event in the tunnel under the stadium making the dish for the dive. Kris, who was prone to whine about his difficult assignments but would always deliver, came to me midway through the day to say it couldn't be done. "As fast as I pile it up, it melts," he exclaimed, pointing out the futility of such a project in the middle of July. However, when the time came, Kris was ready.

Skinny Bobby was introduced during the pregame show and walked out on the field shirtless and in cutoff jeans. A diving board was assembled on the back of a pickup truck. Onto the field came another truck pulling a flatbed trailer with a giant ice cream sundae. Kris had bought a child's plastic swimming pool for a dish, filled the bottom of it with foam rubber (to take up space) and piled it high with ice cream. He bought cases of Miracle Whip topping to put over the ice cream, covered it all with chocolate syrup, and topped it off with a red beach ball in place of a cherry. It looked real.

As the crowd encouraged him, Skinny Bobby climbed the ladder and walked to the tip of the diving board, looking down at the ice cream concoction. A couple of times he acted as if he wouldn't jump. The crowd booed. But finally he made the big leap. Head first, he splashed into the vanilla ice cream, whipped cream, and chocolate syrup. And then he sank.

Only then did it become evident that a human being cannot swim in ice cream. Take my word for it. The stuff is like quicksand. After waiting a couple of minutes for him to surface, we all dove in and rescued him just in time. Poor Bobby was turning blue but struggled his way out of the dish and waved his arms in celebration to the applauding crowd.

By the time the flatbed trailer was pulled off the field for the game, ice cream was everywhere, melting all over the ground. The Braves played that night on an infield that was considerably messier and much stickier than usual.

Ice cream wasn't the only food we used in promotions. For Wishbone Salad Dressing, we allowed fans to scramble through the world's largest salad at home plate in an effort to win a car. Actually, it wasn't a real salad. We used rolls of light green newsprint and wadded it up to look like lettuce. That, too, was Kris Krebs's job. Truckloads of this make-believe lettuce were placed on home plate and topped with Wishbone Salad Dressing. There was no container for the salad. It was dumped right on the field.

Then three "lucky fans" were selected at random from the crowd to scramble through the salad and try to find the right key to a new car sitting on the infield. "Lucky fans" was my term. They might not have felt so lucky. We had several keys in the salad, and every once in a while one of the scramblers would crawl out to the salad, tired, sweaty, covered in salad dressing, and holding a key, only to find that the key didn't fit the car. Eventually a victor emerged.

Lucky fans scrambling around the infield became an element of many of our promotions. A favorite was the $25,000 Cash Scramble, which sounds a lot better than it really is. Basically, we wadded up $25,000 in dollar bills and picked a half-dozen people out of the stands who got to stuff as much money into their clothes as they could in ninety seconds of scrambling. In reality, it was possible to grab only three or four hundred dollars in that amount of time. We could have had a $100,000 Cash Scramble or even a Million Dollar Cash Scramble and it wouldn't have cost us any more money.

The magic of the cash scramble was that it was always good for some terrific wire service photos, particularly if you were lucky enough to have a couple of photogenic kids and also some pretty young women in shorts and halter-tops participating. Not that luck actually had anything to do with it. Even though we allowed everyone entering the game to register, Kris would be dispatched to the stands to make sure the contestants had the look we wanted.

We got a lot of hype out of the Cash Scramble and it didn't cost us much money, so we did it several times during the season. We made the most of it. When the scramble was about to start, security guards would march out and surround the field. Once we even had the National Guard with rifles and bayonets. We then had a Brinks armored truck drive on the field, and the Brinks guards would take the bags of money from the back and spread the crumpled bills all over the infield. All the security wasn't necessary since we used play money, but nobody knew that but us. We originally used real money but it took too long to uncrumple the leftovers, so we began using the phony money and then redeeming it for the real thing.

One night during the promotion, a man jumped over the top of the dugout and rushed the field. He fought his way through the line of security, risking his life in an attempt to get at the bonanza of bills on the field. He was arrested, but only after he realized he was going to jail for grabbing phony loot.

Big bucks giveaway: The $25,000 Cash Scramble.

It amazed me how people would sacrifice every inhibition when they participated in the Cash Scramble. Shy kids would jump right in. Even the most reserved ladies would be wildly stuffing money into every crevice of their clothing. Twice young women took off their blouses and stood topless in front of the baseball crowd while shaking the money out of their clothes. The entire crowd could see just how crinkled their bodies were after stuffing so much crumpled money inside their clothing.

Once the season got underway we were determined to have at least some kind of promotional event every single game. That presented two basic problems. It got tougher and tougher to come up with something different. And sometimes promotions got doubled up on each other.

In May we put a home-plate wedding on the schedule as our promotion for Sunday, July 11. The problem was we didn't have a couple to get married. Kris Krebs was assigned to conduct a search, and we also started advertising on the stadium message board and the radio broadcasts: couple needed for home-plate wedding.

Kris, of course, complained that there was no way we would ever find anyone, but then immediately he started coming back with names. One couple called in and volunteered. Then another. And another. Soon we had a dozen. How would we ever choose? We decided to go ahead and let all the people who responded get married that day. In fact, we were curious about just how many we could find.

In the meantime, Ted promised his friend Jim Barnett, who owned Georgia Championship Wrestling, that we'd have a wrestling day at a Braves game. The rink would be set up on the field, and they'd televise wrestling live, right from a Braves game at the stadium. The only day available was July 11—the same day as the weddings.

We met to decide what to do in our predicament, to determine which promotion would be cancelled or moved. It was difficult to tell people they had to change their wedding day once they'd planned on it. And the only open day on the wrestling schedule was that Sunday. Figuring there was nothing really incompatible about weddings and wrestling, we decided to have them both. The weddings would take place at home plate before the game, the wrestling would be after. We'd promote it as "Wedlock and Headlock Day."

As the day approached, the excitement and the crowd were building. We had thirty-four couples scheduled to get married and all the accompanying groomsmen, bridesmaids, and other attendants. We'd literally have hundreds of people on the field for the ceremony. The next big project for Kris was to find an official to marry them. He called every church and could find no willing pastor. He finally found a justice of the peace who ran a wedding chapel on the side. Barring rain, we were set.

When the day came, the sky was clear and the event was spectacular. All the brides had on their white dresses, and one of the trains was even made of Braves pennants sewn together. Each wedding party's bridesmaids had their own

Wrasslin' to follow on Wedlock and Headlock Day.

distinct dresses, and all the grooms and groomsmen wore tails. Ted even kept his shirt on during the ceremony.

Unlike the players on most other big-league clubs, who often balk when asked to participate in promotions, ours didn't even have to be asked. When the organist started playing the wedding music, the Braves players formed in two lines to make a tunnel of crossed bats from home plate to the pitcher's mound. Each wedding party marched with pomp and ceremony under the crossed bats. Granted, it was a little more difficult to hold a Louisville Slugger high in one outstretched hand than the players anticipated, and they kept switching from hand to hand to relieve the strain, but the scene made spectacular photography for both the wedding albums and the sports press.

As for the wrestling, it went without a hitch. The rink was set up in the first-base picnic area, and TV cameras rolled as Braves and Mets players joined the fans after the game to watch. Wedlock and Headlock Day had been a success. Now there was no limit to the number of promotions we could have at once.

The Braves games were the perfect setting for anything we wanted to do. We paid the legendary wire-walker Karl Wallenda $3,000 to walk his wire across the top of the stadium between games of a doubleheader. The stunt was the most amazing I could imagine. Basically, the Great Wallenda, as he was called by those who follow wire-walking, drove into town with all his equipment in the back of a truck. He, his niece, and a couple of other family members strung the wire (actually a cable) across the very top of the stadium, spanning over first and third base from the stadium light towers, more than three hundred feet across. Wallenda was in his seventies, but he worked the entire day prior to the walk putting up the contraption.

In fact, the night before his performance Wallenda was so tired that he fell asleep during the game on a sofa in the press lounge adjacent to the press box. Dozing off is likely what any seventy-year-old man who had just been through a day of hard

The Great Wallenda walks the wire above the stadium.

labor might do. But he had taken a few drinks, and rumor swept through the press box that he passed out drunk. The old man, so they thought, was in a stupor, and the next day I was paying him to walk a long, thin wire a hundred feet above the ground in a stadium full of people, many of them kids. Everyone assured me he would fall and kill himself in front of all those people. And, of course, it would be my fault.

Perplexed, I decided to climb into the lights of the stadium and try to comprehend just what Wallenda had in front of him the next day. I wanted to take a close look at the wire Wallenda would have between him and the ground. I'll always remember the moment I stood at the edge of the wire and looked down on the field and crowd below. I tried to imagine what it would take to make that first step out onto the wire. The ball game was going on below, and the players looked like little bugs moving around. The crowd was a mass of blurry spots. It was terrifying. No way this could be done.

During the first game of the doubleheader the next day, Ted called me to join him in his seats next to the dugout. "I know winds," Ted said in an obvious reference to his sailing, "and these are the most dangerous kinds. Cancel the old man's walk. Tell him it's too risky."

I tried to talk Wallenda out of walking, but his reputation was at stake. Circus performers are legendary for their determination that "the show must go on."

The whole scenario of the Wallenda walk was deadly. At the end of the first game of the doubleheader, every able-bodied ground-crew member and stadium usher was on the field. They faced each other in two lines parallel to Wallenda's cable, and each one was given the end of one of the many ropes attached to the cable. Each man wrapped his rope-end around his waist twice and knotted it in front, then leaned backward to provide enough tension to keep the cable steady. No one could slip, they were told, or the Great Wallenda would fall.

"Oh, God," I thought to myself, "I've finally killed someone. I've gone too far."

Wallenda, looking every bit his age, stepped onto the cable. The crowd gasped as he walked slowly, holding onto a long balance pole, crossing the stadium a step at a time. Every few steps he would stop and look like he might be stumbling or losing his balance. He would yell instructions down to the ground. But by the mid-point of his walk, I could tell this guy knew what he was doing. On closer look, the uncertain steps looked more act than accident. And in twelve minutes flat, he was all the way across, safe on the other side.

He was an amazing man. Performing was his life, and after that first frightful performance, I had him back to repeat several times. "Walking the wire is living," he would say. "Everything else is waiting."

When news reports came in 1977 that he had died in a fall in Puerto Rico, all of us at the Braves were saddened to lose a friend. We had a real appreciation for his culture and pride as a performer. He proved just what greatness could be achieved by someone who devoted a lifetime to a single, difficult skill.

It never crossed my mind that anyone else could do what Wallenda did, but the Braves had established a reputation for wild promotions, and people were calling us daily with new stunts they offered to perform. All they wanted in return was the chance for their big break.

14

NEVER TRUST A FREE DAREDEVIL

One night I was in my office overlooking the stadium field while a game was going on. The switchboard operator called and said someone was in the lobby to see me. The someone was Jay Cochrane, a wire-walker who had come all the way from Canada because he understood I was the person most likely to give him his big opportunity. He had grown up as an admirer of Karl Wallenda and wanted to duplicate his walk across the top of our stadium. He'd do it for free.

Now the name Jay Cochrane just didn't have the daredevil ring of Wallenda. I couldn't imagine people getting excited about "The Great Cochrane." I was skeptical. Nevertheless, the Great Cochrane took me to his trailer and showed me his equipment. I knew enough to realize it was basically the same stuff Wallenda used. He explained to me the type of greaseless cable he used, the way he would secure it, and the method of stabilizing it on the ground with men holding ropes. I knew I had heard the same explanation from Wallenda.

Back in my office, Jay showed me his scrapbooks. He was indeed a professional wire-walker, with news reports from Canada about his walks between buildings. Still, I told him I was very uncomfortable. It was late in the season, and the Braves were so far out of the pennant race that nothing would draw a crowd. I had no money to pay him and didn't want anyone to risk his life for free. Besides, the only game we could do it was just a week away, leaving no time to promote the event adequately.

His argument was simple. He had driven all the way from Canada for the break of a lifetime. I was either going to give him that break or let him down. He'd give me until the next day to think about it.

I called every reference I could find — circus performers who knew Jay Cochrane, event promoters who had hired him in the past, newspaper writers who covered his Canadian walks. All reported he was great, that he could perform the walk in Atlanta, so I decided to let him go ahead with it.

We promoted the walk as much as we could with just one week's notice. We blared it over radio and television and took a couple of ads in the paper. "The New Wallenda" would walk. On the day of the game Jay had everything in place, much more organized than Wallenda had ever been. When the time came, the crowd was small but excited.

Our aspiring Wallenda, in his nifty sequinned outfit, told me he had a real surprise for the crowd. When he reached the mid-point of his walk, he would stand on his head, balancing atop his balance pole. Then he would press a button and fireworks would erupt from each end of the pole. This looked like it might be even better than Wallenda.

The moment arrived. With his first step, I knew I was in trouble. Not only would he not be able to stand on his head half-way across; it didn't look like he would make it that far in the first place. Every step was a struggle. The difference between Wallenda's fake false steps and the real false steps that our new walker was taking became all too obvious.

Most of the crowd was leaving. I wanted to. Nobody wanted to be there when he fell. By the time he reached midway, after twenty minutes of effort, it was clear he would have no desire to attempt a headstand. However, pride stepped in, and instead of his head, he went down on one knee. Then he pushed the button on his pole, but only the fireworks on one end went off. Worse, the pole was blasted right out of his hands. There he was clinging to the cable for his life.

During the next half-hour, he inched his way across the remaining portion of the cable. By this time, all faint-hearted fans had left the stadium. A brave few watched in fear to see if Jay Cochrane would make it. He completed the performance, but inspired me to send a memo the next day, informing my staff of the only iron-clad rule I would ever set for our promotions: "Never trust a free daredevil."

Sometimes it was hard to obey my rule. The lines between daredevil and good fun are just too fuzzy. Once a man showed up at my office and asked to be given the chance to jump over twenty-one buses on a special motorcycle he had built. It was propelled by rockets. I listened and was intrigued. He had jumped fifteen buses at state fairs on a regular motorcycle, and ours would be the first public attempt by him or anyone else on a jet-propelled cycle. It certainly seemed like something that would draw a crowd.

He invited me to walk with him to the hotel across from the stadium, where the cycle was on display in the lobby. It was shiny, black, and trimmed in red and silver stripes. It was beautiful. Its sleek lines made it look something like a jet fighter sitting on two motorcycle wheels. It had small fins on the back like an airplane, and the jet-engine cylinders also protruded from the back.

I was impressed and about to consider his offer. After all, he had looked at all his options and decided to unveil his act before one of our games . . . and was willing to do it for free.

"This thing must be hard to ride," I said. "How many times have you jumped on it?"

He gave me an incredulous look and explained he couldn't possibly test-drive the machine. "It would be too dangerous. I might get killed." He was saving himself for the stadium jump. The temptation to give him his chance vanished.

Another time, a man named Wayne Smith came to my office. He wanted his big break, too. His trick was to hang upside down from a crane fifty feet above the ground and escape from a straitjacket. He would do it for free. I told him no — free daredevils were not allowed. We had a rule.

He begged. Finally I agreed to give him a chance. I figured the worse thing that could happen would be for him to hang upside down and not be able to escape. Then we would just lower him back to the ground. No way anything really bad could happen.

We scheduled his trick between games of a Braves-Reds doubleheader. When the first game ended, a huge crane started onto the field from the right-field gate. Sylvia Adamson, my promotions assistant, had traded eight tickets for the use of the crane, plus driver. It was the biggest crane I had ever seen in my life. There are normally about twenty minutes between games. It took the crane longer than that to set up. It dug its way through the outfield turf en route to home plate.

We had altered Wayne Smith's name slightly to "Houdini Smith" for the sake of better promotion and had graciously agreed to pay him fifty dollars to buy a new suit for his performance. I was pretty impressed. The giant crane was awesome. As it cut its swath through the stadium grass, I knew our groundskeeper wouldn't be pleased. But I would be excused because of the delight over this great spectacle.

Marshall Mann, our public-address announcer whose deep, bellowing voice sounds like God must sound, gave the introduction. "Ladies and gentlemen, tonight you will witness one of the most incredible feats ever attempted at a major-league baseball stadium. Introducing the world-famous daredevil . . . the great escape artist . . . Houdini Smith."

Houdini came running onto the field from the Braves' dugout in his new light-green leisure suit (not what I was expecting him to wear), and instantly our players ran onto the field to put the straitjacket on him, wrap him in chains, and hook his feet securely. He was ready to be hoisted fifty feet above the stadium turf for his great escape. I was still impressed.

The crane had lifted him about five inches above the ground when his face turned beet-red and he started yelling, "I'm having a heart attack!"

He immediately escaped from the chains and jacket and the crane lowered him from his spot inches above the grass. I could hear the players wisecracking in the background. "Did that look like fifty feet to you?" Phil Niekro asked. "Didn't look like fifty feet to me."

The crane dug another pair of trenches as it burrowed its way off the stadium field, and the groundskeepers spent the next few minutes filling in the ruts with sand and smoothing out the field as best they could.

Houdini lived, by the way. I seriously considered changing that fate, especially after I found out he was suing the Braves because his hair fell out due to the trauma of the event. Once again I laid down my law: never, never trust a free daredevil.

15

LIFE WITH TED

"Bob, Ted needs to talk to you." It was Dee Woods, Ted's secretary. Dee is a wonderful woman. She was essential to all of us who had to deal with Ted daily. She kept his schedule, checked things out for us, and virtually could read his mind. In fact, when Ted left the office, Dee would give him an index card that listed everything he was to do that day. All he had to do was check the card. She kept order in his life.

Whenever I'd hear those seven words from her on the phone, I'd cringe with anxiety. Ted Turner's raspy, twangy voice was about to come on the line, and the conversation was likely to be from outer space.

"Hope, you don't like me, do you?" he asked one time.

"Sure I like you, Ted," I answered.

"I know you don't like me," he continued. "You never come to sit with me during games."

"Ted, I like you fine. Besides, I don't have to like you. You're the boss. I respect you."

"Respect's not the same as like," he'd bark and hang up.

It was one more in the daily series of strange phone calls from Ted.

"Hope, you're always honest with me," he said this time. "Tell me the truth. What's wrong with the Braves? Why aren't we winning?"

"Do you really want to know, Ted?"

"Yeah, tell me the truth. I can take it."

"Well, Ted, someday you need to realize we just have a bad team."

"You can't say that," he screamed into the phone. "That's like telling me my kids are ugly. You're through. That's it for you. You're fired."

My firing lasted through the weekend, and then when I went to see him about it on Monday, he said almost meekly, "Oh, that. That wasn't anything."

"It sounded like something to me," I said.

"Ah, Hope," he said, rolling his head around, "I was just joking."

He wasn't joking, but that was life with Ted Turner.

His moods changed with the wind. He was the smartest man I'd ever met, and he was also the dumbest, depending on when I was with him. He was always running full tilt.

I'd walk into his office for a meeting and sit down in front of his desk. His office at the TV station was a trophy case; it wasn't large, but the entire wall to the left as you faced his desk was a bookcase filled with silver trays and sailing cups. Other sailing trophies and momentos covered the credenza behind his desk and a table along the left side. The desk itself was always amazingly clean compared to the relative untidiness of the rest of the place. It just had a phone and a small billboard reading, "Lead, follow, or get out of the way" — Ted's favorite motto. On the table beside his desk was a photo of his wife Janie sitting on the deck of a boat.

When I'd sit down in one of the two leather chairs in front of his desk, he'd look me straight in the eye. I knew immediately he was trying to stare me down. He wasn't going to blink until I blinked. He wouldn't turn his head away until I turned mine. It was his effort at some strange kind of mind control, and I was the subject.

A couple of other people might be in the room watching as Ted and I sat there just looking at each other, not saying a word. The contest could last several minutes, with Ted to get control and me fighting against it. Finally, both of us would give in at a delicately orchestrated moment, never quite sure which one had won or lost.

He would never say a word about it, and I never saw him go through that routine with anyone else. Once he told me I frustrated him because I did whatever I wanted to regardless of what he thought. I considered that a compliment, although I'm not sure he meant it that way.

The staring game was an example of one of his specialties — winning psychological battles with the people around him. At Braves games, he'd jump up and down cheering. Rising to his feet and sitting back down, he'd test whoever was sitting with him. If the person jumped when Ted jumped, that person was a follower, someone Ted could control. Usually, if the game lasted long enough, he would have almost any of his guests jumping up and down in unison following his lead.

Once Walter Dunn, who was in charge of buying sports advertising for the Coca-Cola Company, was planning his trip to a game with Ted. He asked me what to expect. I told him about Ted's jumping act. I watched during the game as Ted started standing and applauding. Walter never budged. Ted then started jumping up and down a little more. Walter still stayed put. I could tell Ted was getting frustrated. He'd stand up, sit down, stand up, sit down, then look over his shoulder to see if Walter was responding. Ted just couldn't make any headway.

During the game, I saw Walter on the concourse. He looked at me smiling and asked, "How am I doing?" I told him he was doing great. "It's not as easy as it looks," he responded.

Ted considered himself the greatest promoter on earth, and I was *his* promoter. That seemed to produce a strange alliance between us. Both of us believed in high-profile promotions and both pushed hard, but we both had our own opinions as to how things should be done. That frequently caused disagreements, but on the other hand, many people at the TV station and on the team would work through me when they really needed something from Ted. They thought I had his respect if not his friendship.

Some people around him were obviously close friends, and Ted liked having them close. Terry McGuirk was a recent college graduate who hung around Ted everywhere he went. Terry had spent summers researching cable-television systems. Cable TV had been around for years, mostly acting as a central antenna and helping people in small, remote communities pick up the signals of TV stations from the nearest big city. The big television stations were lobbying heavily to make this practice illegal since they got no compensation from the cable systems for their "pirated" signals. They supplied the programming and got nothing in return. Ted had a theory that someday the FCC would deregulate the "pirating" of station signals and a small station could then be seen across the nation like one of the three big networks. If that were to happen, the pirated station would be able to make its money from increased advertising revenue because more people would be watching. It was a theory Ted was going to test. Buying the Braves complemented his movie library by providing him with five hundred more hours of TV programming. Movies and sports. It would be the perfect combination for the first national cable TV station. In fact, with so many Braves games being televised from coast to coast, it would become "America's Team."

McGuirk was a bright, tall, good-looking young man who became a very close friend of Ted's during all this research. Also, Ted sent him to work in the Braves' office as a "spy" for a few months after he bought the team. It was Ted's practice always to put an insider into new operations to give him better insight about what was going on. McGuirk was even sent to spring training to practice with the Braves the first spring.

Gerry Hogan seemed to be Ted's favorite among his highest-ranking staff. Gerry, in his early thirties, was general sales manager of the station. Gerry and Terry both had soothing effects on Ted's mercurial personality. When Ted blew, they could calm him down. Ted and I had shouting matches over almost any issue, but Gerry was my close friend and I'd rely on him to calm the storm. Ted would turn over responsibility for new parts of the organization to me one day, then yell at me for being an "empire builder" the next. Gerry would explain to Ted that I hadn't asked for the new challenges, but that he had assigned them to me. Gerry and Terry were Ted's two closest associates inside the company.

Al Thornwell, Perry Bass, Ted Munchak, Bud Seretean, Bruce Wilson, Mike Gearon, and others fell into the category of wealthy associates. Ted said the best way to get rich is to hang around rich people. These were his rich people.

Ted particularly liked rich people who he thought could help his business. Bud Seretean started Coronet Mills, a carpet company in Dalton, Georgia, and sold it to RCA, becoming the largest single shareholder of that company. RCA made and installed earth stations, an essential part of the equipment necessary to transmit a television signal by satellite.

Perry Bass, an oil billionaire from Fort Worth, was a sailing friend. Once, when I was sitting in Ted's office, he interrupted the meeting to talk to Bass on the phone. "Never let someone worth a billion bucks wait," Ted smiled after borrowing some money from him to tide things over until the situation with the Braves got better.

One morning I awoke to a phone call from Ted, asking me to come to his office immediately. It was early morning, and Ted had called me at home only a couple of other times, both at night after he had first bought the team. I showed up at the television station around seven-thirty, and the place was deserted. Channel 17, at that time, was hardly a showcase. I drove into the parking lot next to the plain, two-story red building. The parking lot was small, usually without enough space for all the cars. It surrounded a small, single-story building that was the base for his giant broadcast tower. The roof of the building and everything else nearby were covered with auto tires, protection from objects falling from the tower. Parking in the lot never left me with a safe feeling. My car didn't have tires on top, and I was always glad to find it in one piece when I got back. This particular morning the lot was empty except for Ted's Toyota. Even though the TV station operated all night, it basically ran itself. The film projectors operated automatically to keep the movies running. That was about it. So on this morning, Ted and I may have been the only ones around.

I went in the side door of the station, walked up the steps and peeked around the corner to check Ted's desk. He was sitting behind it, tie loose and hair uncombed. He looked like he had been there all night.

"Come on in. Sit down," he ordered. "You think I'm crazy, don't you?" he asked in a very concerned voice.

I was uncomfortable coming to see him anyway, but now I was really uncomfortable. It must have showed.

"Don't get nervous. I'm not mad," he said. "I just know you think I'm crazy. I can tell by the way you look at me sometimes."

I chose my words carefully. "Well, Ted, there's good crazy and there's bad crazy," I explained. "You have to admit you're not exactly like anyone else. But I don't think you're going to hurt anybody or anything like that."

I waited for his response, wondering if I had said the right thing. Joe Shirley, who was in charge of stadium security, had told me that Ted kept a gun in the right-hand top drawer of his desk. I was hoping he wouldn't move in that direction. None of us was ever certain what Ted might do. He regularly talked about killing himself, and everyone was well aware that his father had committed suicide. We assured ourselves he was only joking, but we were never sure. He talked about it too much.

"I've been worrying about what you think of me," he continued.

This can't be for real, I thought to myself.

"I am crazy and I want to tell you why," he went on. "When I was a boy, my sister had lupus. My parents had to keep her locked in her room, and I'd walk by and listen through the door. I'd hear her banging her head against the wall in pain, screaming, 'God, let me die; God, let me die.'

"When she died, my mother couldn't take it. Don't get me wrong, I love the woman. But she's never gotten over it.

"My father . . . I loved my father," he continued. "I was never sure if he loved me. He sent me off to boarding school. I'd do anything to please him but never thought I could. Finally, when I left college and started working with him at the outdoor company, we were getting along great. I thought everything was fine. Then I got a call one day that he'd killed himself.

"Hope," he concluded in a soft voice, "I may be crazy, but I wanted you to know why."

I kept thinking during his explanation that I couldn't imagine feeling sorry for him, but at that moment I did.

Immediately he shifted gears and asked me what I thought of Tal Smith, the general manager of the Houston Astros. We talked for the next few minutes about baseball, as if the earlier conversation had never taken place. Then he summarily ended the meeting just as quickly as it had begun.

Ted was an unusual but effective teacher. He'd give us insight into his wisdom and planning, and I was frequently the recipient of his philosophical insights because I was so young and easy to impress. He felt he had to let a few people in on what he was really thinking; they would later be able to testify as to his genius. I was around him virtually every day, so I felt I had him figured reasonably well. Most people would say they couldn't tell when he was serious and when he was putting on an act. I was certain I could tell.

Sometimes he would walk into my office and start pacing back and forth, rattling on about any number of subjects. He was like an actor rehearsing his lines. The next couple of weeks I would hear the same speech over and over at public gatherings. Then he'd change his material, and I'd be the rehearsal audience again.

Many of his lines were trite but right. "Many hands make light work," he would say, encouraging us to work together to get a particular task done. "A faint heart never won a fair maiden," he'd declaim when pushing us to call prospective advertisers. He constantly complained about the rich and pompous "muckety-mucks" he had to deal with in business, as if he were impoverished and struggling under their influence.

Occasionally, he'd do something to infuriate me. Once, at a reception in the Stadium Club, I heard Ted asking for me. In his impatience, he asked, "Where's Hope? Where's that idiot Hope?" I went to his rescue but was burning.

The next morning I charged to his office, only to be told he was busy and would call me later. Later in the day he came bouncing into my office.

"Hope, what do you want, pal?" he chirped.

I was still mad. I got up out of my chair, walked around the desk, and shut the door. Then I placed the first finger of my right hand straight into his chest, pushing him against the door.

"Don't you ever say anything like that again in public about me," I warned. I knew at once he had no idea what I was talking about.

When I explained, he was profuse in his apologies. "I call people that all the time. It doesn't mean anything. You're one of my best friends. I was nervous. I say all kinds of strange things. I don't even know what I'm saying sometimes."

For the next two weeks, everywhere we went, Ted was calling his friends, almost everyone he met, "idiots." Only Ted could make "idiot" sound like an acceptable greeting.

He also invited me to join his sailing crew, "the ultimate sign of friendship." I turned down that opportunity since I had never sailed in my life. I had a nagging feeling that if I fell overboard, I might have to swim to shore.

Ted's desire to be famous was unabashed. Once, when we were walking through the Charlotte airport, he turned to me and asked if I thought people recognized him. He wanted to be recognized, but he also realized that wasn't enough.

"Hope," he said, "all I ever wanted was to be rich and famous. Now everybody knows me and I have more money than I could possibly ever spend, and I'm still not happy."

"Do you know why I like sailing?" he once asked.

"It's your hobby?" I answered.

"Yeah, it's my hobby," he continued. "But do you know why I really like it? I like it because poor people don't sail. If you want to get rich, the best way to get rich is to hang around rich people. Stay close to the ones that you're smarter than and avoid the ones that are smarter than you. That's how you get rich."

One time when I was sitting on a bookcase in his office, he walked up and looked at me from head to toe. "Hope, you're a great promoter, maybe the second-best promoter in the world to me," he said. "You're the only person who works for me who might have been able to do the things I've done. You need a look," he continued. "You look too plain. You need something like my moustache and the gap in my front teeth. That's my look. You need to stand out in a crowd. Think of Hitler. Nobody'd remember what he looked like if he didn't have a moustache. You've got to have your own special look to be great."

Alas, I never developed a look.

One night he took me and sportswriter Wayne Minshew into the bar at the team's hotel to talk. "Someday I'm going to be the first person in the history of the world to be able to talk to everyone," he said. "I'll be able to talk to all the world's leaders and bring peace to the world through television." He then went on to say he'd been thinking about running for president of the United States but now he had more important things to do with his life.

I had strategies for dealing with Ted that seemed to make life easier. Each year I'd write a long, elaborate plan and budget. I'd submit it to Ted for approval. Ted would write "okay by me" on the first page and send it back. I knew he had never read it. So I just went ahead and did whatever I felt like I needed to do. If Ted ever questioned anything, I'd tell him it was in the plan, whether it was or not.

I was promoting furiously and proud of my status as the

widely recognized, free-wheeling, super-salesman of Atlanta, spending money whenever I needed and doing whatever I wanted. My fame may have been modest, but I was proud of it. Whenever *Atlanta* magazine listed the most influential people in the city, "Ted Turner's promoter" Bob Hope was included. The newspapers described me regularly as a promotional "genius." I loved it.

One Saturday morning, I woke up to see a front-page head-line in the *Atlanta Constitution* — "Atlanta's Super Promoter" — over a photo of me. There I was in a front-page newspaper story telling the world I was the best. I was proud. Let's face it, I thought, I'm pretty hot stuff.

A few days later I was in Ted's office when he reached over and opened the top right-hand drawer of his desk. At first I thought he was going for the gun Joe Shirley had told me about. Then I saw him pull out a newspaper, and as he opened it, I knew exactly what day's paper it was.

"Hope," Ted said, pointing to my front-page story. "I've given you a lot of freedom, as much freedom as any employee I've ever had. I've let you spend whatever money you need and do whatever you want to do. Don't you ever forget who's boss and whose money you're spending."

I still had some things to learn about Ted.

16

TED'S FIRST OFF-SEASON

In 1976, the Braves nearly doubled the previous year's attendance despite the team's first last-place season. Ted Turner and his refreshing attitude about the Braves created a lot of excitement in the South. Fans had confidence he was committed and would build a winning team.

The promotions during the year ranged from occasionally sublime to frequently ridiculous. Ted was overzealous in his attempt to put nicknames on the backs of the players' shirts. The National League didn't accept his explanation that "Channel" was Andy Messersmith's nickname when placed over his uniform number "17." It looked too much like a "Channel 17" advertisement. Messersmith's shirt nickname was quickly changed to "Bluto," which didn't suit a shaggy blonde-haired Californian any better than "Channel 17."

Spaghetti and pizza were served to all fans on the field after games, and although this kind of promotion may not have drawn big crowds, it didn't cause any problems, either. We were having fun. Even serving champagne to all fans following the season-ending game, a no-hitter pitched by San Francisco's pitcher John Montefusco, proved harmless enough.

Despite the last-place finish and the goofiness of the year, most baseball experts felt 1976 had more positives than negatives. The team was heading in the right direction, but some baseball executives were wary of Ted Turner.

No question about it, Turner was the fans' owner. When the team played poorly, he made no excuses. He said it was bad. When he did something wrong, he admitted it. When the Braves did something good, he was the first to jump up and cheer. He had a real knack for saying just what the fans wanted to hear. He was their kind of guy. He also attended every game during his first season as owner. People expected him to be there. He was as much a part of the attraction as any of the players.

During that first season, Ted was involved in everything. He made all the player decisions, despite not knowing much about baseball. A typical day would have him making speeches at breakfast and lunch, selling TV time in the morning, making player moves in the afternoon, participating in some wild pre-game promotion before the game, and then posing for photos and talking to the fans during the games. He was busy. More to the point, he was an active and visible part of the team — maybe the most visible part of the team.

However, if he was the fans' owner, he was not always the favorite of the owners of other major-league clubs. Although they appreciated the new spark of energy he had brought to the team, his antics seemed to embarrass them. Also, he initiated the distribution of his television signal across the country on cable and was calling Channel 17 a national "SuperStation," which suggested he would be televising the Braves more and more into their franchise territories. And his style was, well, uncomfortable.

A typical reaction of the rest of baseball to Ted was voiced by St. Louis Cardinals announcer Jack Buck during dinner before one game. "Your boss is crazy," Buck told a dinner table full of people, "but he's smart enough that they'll never be able to commit him to an institution. On the other hand, if they ever do, they'll never let him out."

Ted was well aware he had a last-place team and was determined to change that. He wanted to convince outfielder Gary Matthews to sign with the Braves when his contract with the

Giants expired at the end of the 1976 season. However, Ted didn't abide by the procedure of waiting until Matthews was free from his Giants contract and available to start talking. In baseball, what Ted did was considered tampering.

At a party for baseball officials, Ted yelled a remark to San Francisco owner Bob Lurie to the effect that Atlanta would offer Matthews whatever it took to sign him. The remark made the newspapers and infuriated Commissioner Bowie Kuhn, along with many of the owners. In their minds, it was one more example of Ted's danger to baseball.

The party took place during the World Series, and immediately afterward Ted put his energy behind getting Matthews signed. Gary was invited to Atlanta, and, at a big celebration at the Stadium Club, many of the city's top officials and business leaders encouraged him to become a Brave. The party looked like it had been planned for weeks. When Matthews arrived in the city, billboards on the way from the Atlanta Airport greeted him by name. Atlanta really wanted Gary Matthews, and Ted was doing everything possible to let him know it.

The Matthews party, by the way, was typical Ted. He came to my office late one afternoon to tell me he wanted the 250 most important Atlantans at the Stadium Club the next night for the event. Somehow, as always, we got the job done.

Matthews did sign with the Braves, by the way, but the matter of Ted's tampering didn't go away. Baseball's winter meetings were coming up in Los Angeles, and word was that the commissioner would decide Ted's penalty for the tampering shortly after they were over. The winter meetings would be a good place for Ted to be on his best behavior.

The week before, Ted called me into his office. His office at the stadium was big but not exactly typical for a team president. It had some of the cluttered atmosphere of his TV-station office but none of the trophies. The art on the walls was a reflection of his personality—a hodgepodge of anything and everything. Behind his desk was a painting of some dogs sitting around a table playing cards. To some people it would be junk, but it was given to him by Andy, the seventy-year-old stadium-elevator operator. Ted hung it on the wall and kept it there. During his first season with the Braves, all kinds of organizations gave Ted plaques and trophies. His office was jammed with them.

One trophy had been presented to him by Tom Beebee, the chairman of the board of Delta Air Lines, honoring Ted for his civic contribution of buying the Braves. When Delta decided not to advertise on Braves games the next year, Ted sent the trophy back to Mr. Beebee in protest.

This day Ted wanted to talk to me about his impending punishment by the commissioner of baseball.

"Hope, what do you think he'll do to me?" he asked.

I had no idea.

"I'll tell you what he's going to do," he answered his own question. "He has three choices. He can give Matthews back to the Giants. But he won't do that because that's punishing Matthews. He could fine me, but that won't do him any good. I have plenty of money and would never miss it. I'd pay it and be perfectly happy. Or, he could suspend me," he continued with a twinkle in his eye. "He could kick me out of the game for a whole season. Get me out of the way. He's been wanting to get rid of me. This is his chance to do it for a while."

Ted went on to explain to me that the suspension was exactly what he wanted. "Look," he said. "I've been the fans' owner, the hero of the little guy. They love me. I run the team the way they think they would if they owned it. I come to the games, sit in the stands, drink a few beers, even take my shirt off. I'm 'Mr. Everyman' to them, their pal Ted."

Ted had a potential problem in 1977 that he wouldn't be able to explain easily to his fans. He was going to spend most of the summer competing in the America's Cup. That was not something that fit his down-to-earth, our-kind-of-guy, our-pal-Ted image. People might suddenly realize he was not only rich but also an elitist—a yachtsman. Or even worse, they would realize yachting came first with him since he'd be missing all the baseball games. But he'd found a way out. It had suddenly occurred to him that he'd have to miss all the games if the

Ted — "the hero of the little guy."

Commissioner suspended him for a year. No one could blame him then. He could sail all summer.

So, Ted said, we had to use the winter meetings to make sure Bowie Kuhn was thankful for the opportunity to get Ted Turner out of the way by suspending him from baseball. That was our challenge. The first week in December we headed to Los Angeles intent on earning his suspension on merit, making sure there was no doubt that getting Ted out of the game, if only for a summer, would be in the best interest of the game of baseball.

Ted wasted no time getting started. The first night we were there, Bill Lucas stopped me in the lobby to tell me Ted had been on his hands and knees barking at people in the hotel restaurant. For the next few hours, that seemed like all I heard, bewildered comments from employees of other teams who had either seen or heard about Ted's barking like a dog.

The next three days were the strangest ever with Ted Turner. He was ranting like a San Francisco street preacher, holding court in the lobby of the Los Angeles Hilton. He told people he feared the commissioner of baseball was going to kill him, that he feared for his life. He would ramble incoherently in the lobby for a while and then disappear to his room with a woman he had met at the hotel. Usually, the women with Ted were very nice looking. This one looked hard and fast.

After we had been at the meetings for three days, a radio reporter for Associated Press cornered me in the hotel lobby and pulled me aside to listen to a bizarre interview Ted had given him. "I don't know what to do with this," he said. "I can't run it." It was Ted telling him he was going to get a gun and kill the commissioner before the commissioner got him first. Ted sounded absolutely crazy on the tape, and despite our plan to do whatever was necessary to get him suspended, this was going too far. I decided I needed to do something. I wasn't absolutely certain it was an act anymore.

I headed across the lobby to look for Ted and grabbed Bill Lucas by the arm along the way. "Bill," I said, "Ted's lost his mind. It's time for us to do something." Bill, who'd been watching Ted perform in the lobby, didn't disagree.

Bill and I had both gone well beyond worrying about our jobs. I was going to have to let Ted have a piece of my mind. We each took one of Ted's arms and pulled him to the escalator leading down to the side doors of the hotel. Next to the entrance was a small bar. We took him in and sat him down. Tagging along behind was his lady friend. I looked Ted square in the eyes and prepared for him to strike back. "Ted," I said firmly, "there's a fine line between being outrageous and being absolutely out of your mind. You've gone over that line."

His lady friend kept trying to interrupt, saying we couldn't talk to Ted that way. He was the boss. But Ted sat there calmly.

"Do you think I should get on a plane and fly back to Atlanta?" he asked.

"Yes, if you can't get your mind together and act right," I said.

"Do you think I've convinced him I'm crazy?" he asked with a smile.

"Yes," I answered. He'd also convinced me.

"I'm okay. I'll behave," he said. He did. For the next couple of days he was fine, perfectly normal.

The next week we returned to Atlanta, and a month later the announcement was made by the commissioner's office. Bowie Kuhn fined Ted $35,000 for tampering with Gary Matthews while he was a Giant, but the commissioner also suspended Ted for the 1977 season.

Fans were incensed. Ted instantly became a martyr. Thousands of fans wrote the commissioner in protest. Burger King even had a promotion offering postcards to send to the Major League Baseball office in New York. Ted used the situation not only to become a hero but also to build a ticket-mailing list. He had us sneak behind the commissioner's back and hire two secretaries in the baseball office to type labels of all the names and addresses of people who sent protest letters and cards. We sent them ticket information.

Ted was undaunted. He had gotten his way. He had become a bigger hero in his hometown, and he had the summer off to sail. He explained to me the advantages of being victimized.

"Hope, always remember, the little guy rises to the big guy's level when they get in a fight," he said. "Take Jesus Christ, for example. He was a poor, unknown preacher until he took on the Roman Empire and lost. They crushed him and then he really got rolling. Like me. I'm rolling now."

Only Ted.

A month later we were planning the Braves' winter caravan, when the players tour towns around the South to promote the upcoming season. Typically, the caravan would hit a town with an autograph session at an indoor shopping mall. Players sat at tables for three or four hours, taking occasional breaks to wander through the mall, shop, and flirt with local women. In fact, on one caravan stop in Rome, Georgia, team manager Bobby Cox met his future wife while roaming the mall. She was selling shoes in a department store, and Bobby just walked up and introduced himself. The direct approach was not unusual. Often the players would take a bag of team buttons and walk up and ask the prettiest women they could find, "Can I pin a Braves button on you?" It wasn't a terrific line but it worked. They made a lot of new friends at every stop.

After an autograph session, the local mayor and a group of team boosters would treat everyone to dinner at the nicest restaurant in town, preceded by a press conference with local writers and broadcasters. The team would spend the night in a local motel and then head to the next town by bus the next morning.

While planning the 1977 caravan, we booked the regular list of towns — Macon, Columbus, Savannah, Augusta, Valdosta, Rome, Gainesville, Albany, and Dalton in Georgia; Chattanooga, Nashville, and Knoxville in Tennessee; and Montgomery, Anniston, Birmingham, Huntsville, and Dothan in Alabama. But a small southwest Georgia town named Plains was in the news that year. Jimmy Carter from Plains was about to become president of the United States. So we decided to make a caravan stop in Plains and selected the Saturday and Sunday before Carter would be inaugurated. We were hoping the Carter family would be spending its last weekend at home.

I was excited about the chance of meeting a president. I had been with Carter many times when he was governor of Georgia, but this would be different. I had never met a president, although I came close during the 1976 All-Star Game in Philadelphia. I was assigned to work in the press box during the game and was pulled aside when I arrived at the stadium. I was told I'd been selected to escort President Gerald Ford to the National and American League All-Star dressing rooms before the game. The Secret Service personnel took me to a stadium office and told me to stay there until they came to get me. Something went wrong. I was left there waiting until well after the game was underway. They had forgotten me, and I'd missed my chance. Now I would have another one.

To book the caravan events in Plains, I called the town hall and asked if they could suggest someone who would help with the local arrangments. Perhaps we could have lunch with a local civic club, sign autographs at the train station, and, if possible, meet the president and his family. I was referred to Maxine Reese, who was the Carter presidential campaign coordinator for Plains. Maxine told me she'd check around town for someone to help me set up the caravan. If she could find someone, she'd call back the next day.

She did call me back and had someone to help. His name was Billy Carter, the president's younger brother. Billy got on the phone and told me not to worry, he'd set up everything. Just give him a couple of days. I told him we'd like to meet his brother and family. He said he'd check it out.

A few days later Billy called back with our schedule. We'd arrive in town at noon and be given an hour-long tour. Then we'd get back on the bus and be taken to the Plains Country Club for lunch. After lunch, we'd go to the high school and play a softball game against the Plains All-Stars. Then we'd end the day with an autograph session at the train station.

I asked Billy if we'd have any time with his brother. He told me he couldn't promise me anything. Ted was counting on meeting Jimmy Carter, and I told Billy I'd be in big trouble if the president wasn't there for Ted. Billy said, "Bob, they won't let me tell you if you're going to meet Jimmy, but tell your Mr. Turner just not to worry about it. You're going to be just fine. Take my word for it." I took his word for it and assumed he meant we were set.

Word of our upcoming trip to Plains spread in a hurry. Usually the caravan consisted of about twenty players, and it was tough talking that many into going. This time we had three buses filled for the trip. All the players on our forty-man winter roster and their families signed up. Everyone in the front office and their families signed up. All the press who covered the team during the season booked to go. In addition to the three buses, we had to add two station wagons and an RV. If we didn't see all the Carters that day, I was in big trouble.

Ted Turner had become a household name by now. The past year as owner of the Braves had rocketed him to fame. But as for his knowing other people, little had changed. He ran in his own circles, and those circles may have included wealthy yachtsmen throughout the world but didn't include most of the political and business leaders in Atlanta and Georgia. Once he asked me to introduce him to the president of the Coca-Cola Company, who came to the ballpark often. And even though Jimmy Carter had been governor and was a friend of virtually every other business leader in Atlanta, Ted had never met him. It was my job to introduce him to my remote acquaintance, the president of the United States.

I had met Governor Jimmy Carter a number of times, since he attended Braves games fairly regularly. Unlike most other politicians, he seldom used the free tickets we offered him. He usually just bought tickets and came to the games unannounced. That was a far cry from the typical politician who delighted in making demands on the team. Once Governor Carter was to participate in a pre-game presentation to Hank Aaron on a Sunday afternoon. He and his daughter, Amy, about six at the time, walked into the stadium through the tunnel entrance and onto the field. After he made his presentation, I noticed he was sitting on the grass with Amy climbing on his back. No one was paying attention. I decided it would be polite to sit with him while he was waiting for the rest of the ceremony to end.

As we sat in front of the dugout on the grass, Carter said he admired the woodcarver who had created a plaque depicting Aaron and Ruth standing together. The woodcarver was Art McKellips of Oregon, and he was participating in the presentation. Governor Carter suggested the woodcarver might be famous some day and asked to have his photo taken with him. I grabbed Mr. Victor, our trusty official Braves photographer, and had a picture of me and Jimmy Carter taken with the craftsman, just in case he became famous.

Ted was nervous all week before the trip to Plains, constantly asking me to make sure I introduced him to President

The Braves' caravan rolls into Plains a few days before President-elect Jimmy Carter's inauguration.

Carter—as if Ted or the new president would go unnoticed in the crowd. I was praying I'd have the chance, that the future first family would show.

Our parade of vehicles pulled into town a little after noon. We stopped and everyone got out, looking around in amazement at how small Plains was. Our one-hour tour might not take more than a few minutes. Maxine Reese greeted us and told us to make ourselves at home and she'd meet us back at the buses when it was time to go to the country club.

It was a long hour. We found Billy Carter's gas station, but they told us Billy wasn't around that day. Ted was getting skeptical.

We finally gathered at the buses, and Maxine led the way to the Plains Country Club. The trip may have lasted thirty seconds. We drove about two hundred yards and pulled off into a field on the right side of the road. The country club wasn't a country club at all. It was an old beat-up shack. A half-dozen people were mingling around when we got there.

Ted jumped off the bus and confronted me to find out what was going on. I was worried myself, but then someone yelled, "There's Billy." Suddenly everyone was rushing up a hill to a row of barbecue pits. Billy Carter came ambling down the hill as we approached. Then we heard a commotion behind us and turned to see a line of limousines pulling in. The entire Carter family stepped out.

The next few hours seemed like a dream. There we were eating barbecue with the next president of the United States. I can remember at one point sitting on the tailgate of a pickup truck, drinking a beer, and eating chicken on a paper plate. I glanced to my left and thought, "That guy sitting next to me is going to be the president on Tuesday."

After lunch, we got back on the buses to go to the high school, where thousands of people surrounded the softball field. It was a bigger crowd than we were used to seeing most nights at Braves games. Our team of big-league players played the Plains All-Stars and lost 17-5. A picture of Hank and Ted presenting a Braves warmup jacket to the president appeared on the front page of almost every U.S. newspaper the next day.

A couple of days later, Al Thornwell told me a secret. Ted said he was going to name me vice president . . . of the Braves, not the United States. Getting Ted together with the president impressed him more than getting him in an ostrich race. It got me promoted.

17

A NEW BRAVES SEASON

The glory of my promotion didn't last long. Ted remembered that we had not sold out his first opening night game and didn't want the same thing to happen in 1977. He wanted to make certain we had a full house, so he came up with an idea — to fire me if the stadium wasn't full. At least that's what he said he would do. I didn't think he'd actually fire me if I failed, but I didn't want to find out.

I gathered my troops, and we jumped right into our plan to fill the stadium. We were unified by our single goal — to save my job. We pulled out all the stops. Opening night had to be a big one.

Usually, a marching band performed on the field before the opening game. We scheduled seventeen bands, knowing they would fill some seats and hoping they had parents and friends who would want to buy tickets to watch them perform. Fireworks drew big crowds for the game on the Fourth of July, so we scheduled fireworks opening night, too.

It was Jimmy Carter's first season as president. Since he was now our pal, we decided to invite him to throw out the first ball and went on to invite all famous Georgians — ranging from announcer Keith Jackson to emcee Bert Parks — to be honored on the field prior to the game. We were doing everything we could to draw a crowd but nothing was working.

How to fill a stadium? Invite seventeen marching bands.

Tickets weren't selling fast enough.

Then we got lucky. When the press learned we had invited President Carter to throw out the first pitch, the story ran in the papers. Then the president sent word he couldn't make it; the story that he was not throwing out the first ball made the papers. He offered his mother, Miss Lillian, to take his place; another story ran. Miss Lillian sent us a letter that she couldn't make it, and that story ran. The newspapers were reporting every move of our efforts to get someone to throw out the first ball of the season.

Pretty soon we caught on. Apparently the best way to get publicity for opening night was to have a lot of famous people turn down our invitations to throw out the first pitch. So we made our list. The newspaper ran the announcement that we invited Queen Elizabeth to do the honors of throwing out the first ball (a great choice, since no one had ever invited her before). Then the newspaper reported that Queen Elizabeth notified us she would not be able to attend. Princess

Ann was pregnant, and she didn't want to leave until the baby came.

We invited King Kong, who had recently starred in a movie about himself. The movie producers sent word that the King was in forty parts in a warehouse in Paris. Besides, he would be too big to fit into the stadium. So he declined our invitation. The newspapers continued to report all the details.

We asked Farrah Fawcett, the biggest star of the time. Her agent notified us she would do it for $50,000. We notified him that if we decided to pay $50,000 to anyone, we'd call her first. Each time, Associated Press and United Press International ran a short report updating our progress . . . or lack of it. The stories appeared all over the country.

Our futile quest for a first-ball thrower became the talk of radio disc jockeys everywhere. I was getting daily calls to be interviewed by stations from Los Angeles to New York. This was an amazing thing. The wilder it got, the more fun people had. But finally the week of opening night arrived and we still didn't have anyone.

Now at the point of desperation, we offered a $500 reward to the person who could come up with the most appropriate famous person to throw out our first ball. People went into a frenzy. My phone never stopped ringing. The White House called. Its switchboard had been swamped, and the president wanted to know if he could send a member of the cabinet. Maybe a couple of members of the cabinet. That wasn't good enough for us. We wanted more.

On the day of the game, the headline on the front of the sports section of the *Atlanta Constitution* read, "Paul Newman to throw out first ball." According to the story, the *Constitution* had learned from an "anonymous tip" that Newman was the thrower. We had never even thought of Paul Newman. He wasn't the one.

When game time arrived, we were sold out. More people than ever had turned out for opening night, but I'm not exactly sure why. More than the regular baseball, they seemed curious about the infamous first baseball. It was an anxious time. They waited with eager anticipation. I'm embarrassed to tell who actually threw out the ball. But I will say that it was the first time in history the cabinet members of the United States of America were booed at a big-league game. They were there in force. In fact, the start of the game was delayed because the United States Attorney General was stuck on the stadium elevator.

Let me say unabashedly, I was proud of myself. I felt I had made something out of nothing. We had created electricity by waving a magic wand. We sold out the game and saved my job at least for the time being.

Ted's suspension wasn't scheduled to start until June 1, and with a successful season opener out of the way, everybody was excited about the prospect of a winning season. But if opening night went well, that was the only thing that did during the first couple of months of the '77 season. The Braves took off on what was beginning to look all too much like the record-setting thirteen-game losing streak of the previous year. When the streak reached seven, Jeff Burroughs, a former American League MVP obtained from the Texas Rangers in the off-season, assured fans not to worry. "One thing's for sure, this team won't lose thirteen games in a row," he said. He was absolutely right. The Braves lost seventeen straight games, breaking their previous record and establishing a new National League mark for pitiful play.

The final loss of the streak was managed by the person with the shortest managing career in baseball history. I was sitting in my office the day after the team lost its sixteenth in a row, when Ted told me he wanted me to write a press release announcing that he was the new manager of the team. He asked what I thought. I told him it was the strangest move he had made yet. The team was in Pittsburgh that day, and Ted was out early, in uniform, running wind sprints in the out-field. His first-hand look at the team as manager didn't last long. The Braves lost that night 2-1, and National League president Chub Feeney ordered him out of the dugout and back up to the front office. The commissioner must have been anxious

A loser in the ostrich derby, Turner looks for revenge in the Motorized Bathtub Race.

for the suspension to start.

With another last-place finish virtually assured just one month into the season, we knew we needed to promote harder than ever. We brought the ostriches and weddings back again. Fans were scrambling on the field more often for more cash. It seemed like every pig in the Southeast was pursued in a greased-pig chase, and every little-leaguer participated in a pregame show. We had Ted racing the broadcasters in motorized bathtubs. He won the bathtub race, by the way. When the National Twins Association was having its convention in Atlanta, we had a pregame game between two teams that were mirror images of each other. We did everything we could think of to create just a little extra excitement for a losing team.

Fireworks always seemed to be a good promotion, so we had fireworks in every way, shape, and form. We had just plain fireworks. We put fireworks to music and called it a Sky Concert. We ran a cable across the top of the stadium and lit fireworks from it, calling the promotion the Japanese Wall of Fire. There was nothing Japanese about it, it was hardly a wall, and it was more like a sparkler than a fire. But big crowds came.

The challenge became to display fireworks in different ways, so we could call it something different each time. One night we decided to have the "End of the World." We would take one standard thirty-minute July-4th-type fireworks show and electrically fire it in a single blast. We asked the fireworks company if they had ever done one that way. They hadn't. None of us knew what to expect.

When the night of the "End of the World" came, we had promoted the event with all the drama we could muster. A dynamite plunger was placed at second base with a fuse running directly to the centerfield wall where the giant blast would be ignited. A "lucky" fan was selected at random to push the plunger when the crowd counted down from ten. Never has a fan been so apprehensive about accepting a prize. When the countdown reached zero, he pushed the plunger, bolted from the field, and jumped all the way up onto the dugout and into the stands. The actual explosion was far less exciting than expected—one loud noise, a lot of smoke, and then silence. The world was still around.

Then, with our backs to the wall, we had the promotion that will probably never be forgotten or forgiven in Atlanta. Of all our hundreds of promotions, this is the one people always throw in our faces, as if it best represented everything we've ever done. I don't think that's the case, but then, I always think the Braves will win too.

First, let me explain. We knew a wet-T-shirt contest was in poor taste and inappropriate for a big-league baseball game, but it really wasn't our idea.

We had a committee of students who helped plan our College Nights for the season. The Braves had just finished the seventeen-game losing streak, and it seemed nothing would get people excited about coming to a game. One of the college students suggested Wet-T-shirt Night. I dismissed the idea.

Totally. Completely. Dismissed. Gone. Rejected.

When I got back to my office after the meeting, someone asked if we had any good ideas. I told them a couple we'd discussed and no one seemed impressed. Jokingly, I mentioned the wet-T-shirt contest, and word instantly spread up and down the halls. Ripples of interest began surfacing. I still had no intention of having the event.

The next day I got a call from Atlanta newspaper columnist Lewis Grizzard. He said he heard we were going to have a wet-T-shirt contest at the stadium. I explained that we had made no such decision, and even though I was certain we wouldn't, I was willing to explore the possibility with someone who cared enough to ask. Interest about anything associated with the Braves was too rare to ignore. He suggested he could write a column about the possibility and ask the readers to respond. The public would decide whether or not it was appropriate to have such a contest. That seemed fair. It wasn't my responsibility to set the moral standards for big-league baseball. So I'd let the readers decide.

Reader response was not conclusive. So Lewis wrote another column specifying the date we were considering for the event. Ticket sales took off. People were buying tickets for an event we weren't even planning to have. In fact, we were pretty certain we could never get away with it, even if we tried.

But when a team is in last place and tickets start selling for a promotion, a strange reasoning process is set in motion. The ridiculous seems plausible, and even the most unreasonable stunt makes sense. Instead of telling people we wouldn't have the wet-T-shirt contest, we started telling them we hadn't made up our minds. In the meantime, we were meeting with local church and community groups to determine if there was any way to make it all right with them.

When we met with the Atlanta Christian Council, they suggested we could have the promotion only if the contest was held after the game, so that anyone who wished to leave could do so. Also, they insisted that a minister representing the group be included as a judge. Honest.

I suspect part of the reason the council even considered the contest was that I was on the committee that year to raise funds for the retired ministers pension. However, we were fast losing our reasons for refusing to hold the promotion. Also, I was beginning to think I might be able to get away with it. My overpowering desire to do something to break out of the doldrums of last place magnified the appeal of the event. Lots of people said we'd never be able to have a wet-T-shirt contest at a big-league game. The churches wouldn't let us do it; baseball wouldn't let us do it; the city wouldn't let us do it. No way. We were ready to tempt fate.

By this time, disc jockeys were talking up the contest on the air and calling to interview me about the promotion. It was picking up a head of steam, developing a life of its own. I'd say, "We're only looking at the possibility. We will only do it if we're convinced it can be done in good taste." Fat chance.

We were now getting calls from a "who's who" list of Atlanta leaders, inviting themselves to be judges. The panel, which eventually outnumbered the contestants, included virtually every major male politician in the city, my brother-in-law, my father, and a host of local businessmen. And, of course, Ted signed up to be a judge.

We had to hold the event . . . or so we reasoned.

Even though a 52,000-seat stadium is hardly the setting to tell whether a T-shirt is wet or not, people were clamoring to attend. At game time, 27,000 fans were on hand, and they waited through a two-and-a-half-hour rain delay before the game ever got started. We discussed with the umpires the possibility of postponing the game because of rain, but the crowd wasn't there to see baseball. A raincheck would be useless.

Frankly, the whole night seemed strange, and since contestants didn't preregister, we were well into the game before we knew whether anyone would enter or not. It was the end of the seventh inning when the public-address announcer asked for all contestants to report to the first-base picnic area. We in the press box waited cautiously to see if anyone would stand

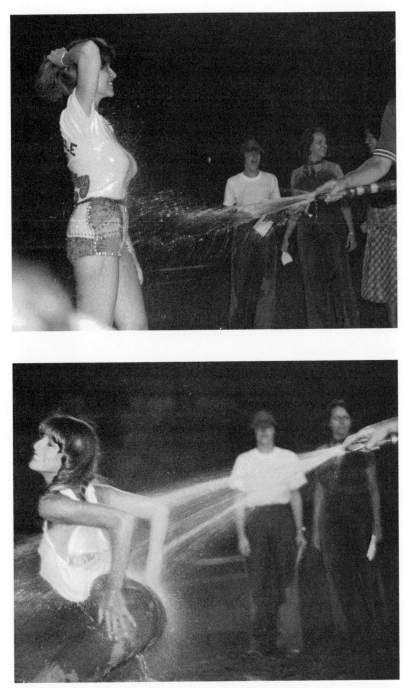

Saying goodbye to good taste: the world's largest wet-T-shirt contest.

and start walking in that direction. For several minutes no one in the stands moved. It was a classic case of nobody wanting to be first. Finally, one young lady stood and started down the aisle. Slowly but steadily the crowd began to applaud. The 27,000 rose to their feet and gave her a standing ovation as she walked down to register. The next forty-two women also got standing ovations as they filed one by one to the registration area.

The game was still in the eighth inning, but no one was paying attention to baseball. The Braves were losing 11-0 to the Chicago Cubs, and Cubs outfielder Bobby Murcer was standing in right field with his glove tucked under his arm, watching the registrations in progress. A routine fly ball dropped near his feet and rolled to the fence. He never saw it until after it hit the ground. He pulled his glove on, ran to pick up the ball, and threw it to the infield. He then returned to the same spot, put his glove back under his arm, and continued to watch the registration.

This was not a real big-league game. It was an oddball dream. Even the players weren't there for baseball. The situation seemed so bizarre that all of us just watched in amazement as the crowd stood and applauded for the final two innings of the game. It was the quietest I had ever seen Ted.

When the game ended, the main event started. The contestants lined up along the first-base line. The ground crew had held an Olympics-type competition the previous day to determine who would have the honor of handling the water hose. They also selected a "touch up" man to work the Windex bottle.

Because of the long rain delay, the contest started at one o'clock in the morning. But even so, the whole Cubs team sat Indian-style, in uniform, along the third-base line and watched the entire competition.

It couldn't happen, but it did. The contest was won by a minister's daughter. Actually, I don't think that was inconsistent with her lifestyle, but her father later called me at home to complain that it hurt her chances to become a United States senator.

Incidentally, the father didn't know she had entered the contest, and definitely didn't realize she'd won until a couple of weeks later. He found out in the worst possible way. She asked to sing the national anthem at a game, and we were happy to oblige. Her father was sitting in the stands watching her sing when someone behind him identified her as the winner of the Braves' wet-T-shirt contest.

The brouhaha didn't end quickly. For weeks, whenever a new team came to town, the players would come by my office to see the contest pictures. Ruhlie Carpenter, the owner of the Phillies, called and wanted a set of the photos sent to him. I thought he was going to send them to the commissioner's office. I would join Ted in being suspended, but in my case the suspension would last forever. It turned out Ruhlie was having them reproduced and sending sets of the copies to his friends.

I readily admit the wet-T-shirt contest was a disgrace. It's hard even for me to understand how we thought we could do it or even why we thought we should do it. It suited the mood of the moment, and that's the way we operated. We'd decide at lunch what we wanted to do, and by mid-afternoon our plans would be so far along that it would be too late to turn back. The Braves were losing, and we were a promotion machine out of control.

We tried everything, though only a few promotions really worked. The fireworks worked. Bat Day and other give-aways to kids worked. And sex-related promotions usually worked.

That's why we decided to introduce the one thousand most beautiful women in Atlanta. We held a contest with Z-93 radio to select them. First we recruited three hundred guys to be judges, and we gave each of them one hundred "finalist" cards to give to the prettiest women they saw. The finalists were invited to the stadium on a Saturday morning for selection of the one thousand winners, who would then be introduced before a game. Most of the pretty women in town got a finalist card everywhere they went. They had handfuls.

About eight thousand women showed up for the finals at the stadium. We picked our thousand, and the game when they were introduced was sold out. Sex had sold another game.

We had a Farrah Fawcett look-alike contest, and the winner received a trip to the All-Star Game, which was in New York at Yankee Stadium. Her homely sister, who went along as a chaperone, tracked me down the second day of the trip, worried that her prize-winning sister had disappeared. I finally found her with John Schuerholz, the farm director of the Kansas City Royals, who was doing a fine job of taking care of her. That was my first meeting with Schuerholz, who turned out to be one of the best general managers in baseball, as well as one of the most innovative and aggressive. It was clear that he also aggressively adhered to Ted's favorite creed, "Faint heart never won fair maiden."

In our effort to dispel the boredom of a long losing season, we tried every strange promotion we could imagine. Once we asked all the local ham radio operators to broadcast into outer space an invitation for flying saucers to land on the field prior to a game. Our theory was simple. If creatures from another world were smart enough to build flying saucers, they would surely be smart enough to pick up our invitation on their radios and to know that landing at a Braves game would be perfectly safe. Hundreds of ham operators participated, stationing their radios high above the stadium in the center-field stands and blasting their message into outer space for weeks. When the game arrived, we felt sure no spaceship would really land, but we weren't nearly so sure as we were when we started the promotion.

In a pregame ceremony, fifty thousand people sat hushed, with the stadium lights turned out and a circle of small lights forming a landing pad on the field. We waited through a spooky few minutes to see if a real spaceship would come. When it didn't, I filled in. I had bought a giant white balloon supposedly shaped like a flying saucer. I filled it with helium and painted it fluorescent green. The big green blob of a spaceship was guided by ropes up over the stadium and pulled down to the field as a blacklight beam focused on it and made it glow. When it reached the small landing pad, a man in a silver suit and space helmet jumped out from under the pad and ran triumphantly around the field. The entire crowd booed. My own mother was ashamed of my hoax, but by this time I didn't care. The stadium was full and I'd take a crowd any way I could get it.

One of the most critical alliances I needed to make dumb promotions work was with our radio and TV announcers. I was blessed in that area. Ernie Johnson, Pete Van Wieren, and Skip Caray were willing to promote almost anything. In fact, Skip was a major contributor to much of my silliness.

One series, when the Braves were playing the Padres and crowds were particularly small, *Atlanta Constitution* sports editor Jesse Outlar wrote that he couldn't understand why Ted Turner televised the games on the SuperStation, which was just beginning to take hold in communities across the nation. Jesse wrote that he was certain no one was watching the games. The next night Skip decided to get even. Skip announced during the game that he was also certain no one was watching, but just in case a few people were, he gave out Jesse Outlar's phone number and asked them to call him. The surge of calls blew out the 572 telephone exchange in Atlanta, making it almost impossible for the newspaper to be printed the next day. With all the lines out, they had no way to get their stories.

Skip also invented Blind Date Night. It wasn't very popular, but he loved it. Fans were invited to send in their photos and Skip would send them free tickets, putting them into a seat next to someone of the opposite sex who also sent a photo. Sadly, a lot of guys would send photos, but only a couple of women. We never quite got Blind Date Night right.

The Braves finally finished the long 1977 season with a 61-101 record. The 101 losses were the most for the team since 1935 when it was in Boston and lost 115. It was the team's second straight season in last place, this time thirty-seven games back. But give our zany promotions their due. Attendance was up for the year despite a team that was only getting worse.

18

A TEAM
DESTINED TO LOSE

The day after the Braves season ended in 1977, I got another call from Ted Turner asking me to come to his office.

"Hope, do you know anything about basketball," he asked.

"No," I answered honestly.

"Great, great," he said. "I want you to go over and run the Hawks."

The Hawks were the Atlanta Hawks, the National Basketball Association team Ted had bought a year earlier. The Hawks season was to start in three weeks and things weren't going very well with them.

"Ted, I don't know anything about basketball," I asserted.

"That's perfect," he said. "I want you to fire everybody in the team's office, cut the team payroll in half, lose every single game, get the number-one draft pick, and then we'll move the team to Charlotte."

"But Ted, I don't know anything about basketball," I said again.

"You don't have to know anything about basketball to lose every game," he stated flatly.

Suddenly, my peaceful baseball off-season turned into a headlong plunge into the quagmire of a struggling basketball franchise. Despite Ted's initial orders, I wasn't completely in charge by any means. Ted asked me to work with Mike

Gearon, a Hawks fan and Atlanta real estate tycoon who agreed to help out without pay.

Ted explained his theory to me. The Hawks had not been successful in Atlanta. He didn't want to be the bad guy if the team was moved out of town. But if the team was bad enough, no one would care. Also, the team with the worst record in the league got the first college draft pick, the best assurance of getting a great player. One great player could turn a basketball team around, he said. All we had to do was lose every game.

I was thrown into the task like a baby pitched into a swimming pool: it was sink or swim. I was now in basketball. I had no other choice.

My first priority was to meet Mike Gearon and the team's coach, Hubie Brown. Mike was in his early forties and retired from developing commercial real estate. In business he had gained the reputation of being something of a strange duck. He generally wore a shirt with no tie, a sports coat, jeans, and Weejun loafers without socks. That was his business uniform. Once I saw him wear a tuxedo to a black-tie dinner, but he didn't wear socks that night either. He was mellow, polite, and constantly spouting theories about virtually every imaginable subject—from how society was overreacting to the dangers of cocaine to psychoanalyses of every human being he had ever met. This penchant for analysis made him an excellent judge of how to improve any organization.

Hubie Brown was also unusual. In his early forties, Hubie had the strongest, most opinionated personality of anyone I'd ever met, including Ted. Hubie had his way of doing things and nothing altered his approach His uniform was a white sailor's cap with the brim turned down, covering his permed, curly grey hair, plus a sports shirt, jeans, and jogging shoes. He had a matching twin, Mike Fratello, as his assistant coach. Mike idolized Hubie, wore exactly the same outfit, and even had the same hairstyle—although Mike was a foot shorter. Both Hubie and his assistant were from the New York area; they had strong accents and an affinity for four-letter words.

Over the next couple of weeks, Mike Gearon and Hubie set

out to cut the team payroll—already the lowest in the league at $1.5 million—in half. Because I still knew nothing about basketball and had enough worry trying to figure out how to get the season started, I kept out of their way.

They made stunning moves. Forward Tom McMillen was obtained from the New York Knicks on the condition the Knicks continue to pay his salary. They signed a five-foot six-inch, thirty-one-year-old rookie guard, Charlie Criss, who had been the leading scorer in minor-league basketball the previous season. They signed rookies Tree Rollins of Clemson and Goose Givens of Kentucky. They almost signed Stan Love, brother of Beach Boys singer Mike Love, on the condition that the Beach Boys would provide a free post-game concert for the Hawks. But the Beach Boys wouldn't agree to terms. All these efforts produced a ragtag front-office operation and a team made up of rejects and rookies.

I set about my task of clearing out the front office, replacing employees with Braves personnel, who, like me, would double up on their jobs. I hesitated to fire the public relations director of the team, a lovely young woman who had just taken the job and moved to Atlanta from Memphis, Tennessee. However, Ted solved that problem by calling me to say he was meeting with her and she had just decided to take a long cruise in the Caribbean. I could hear her crying in the background.

Mike Gearon wasn't the only unpaid worker we had on our staff. During the 1976 baseball season, as Ted was walking through the concourse of Busch Stadium in St. Louis, he was approached by a young law graduate of Columbia University named Stan Kasten. Stan told Ted he was a big baseball fan and would be willing to come to Atlanta and work for the Braves for free. Stan had an office at the stadium and didn't have much work to do. His main occupation seemed to be driving the team's general manager, Bill Lucas, up a wall, and Bill was constantly complaining about Stan's being underfoot. My observation of Stan was that the reason he was underfoot was simply that he didn't have anything to keep him busy. After my assignment to the Hawks, I had lunch with him one day and was impressed by how much he seemed to know about basketball. He certainly knew more than I did. I asked Ted if we could transfer Stan's free salary from the Braves to the Hawks. Ted agreed. Stan soon became basketball's jack-of-all-trades, doing everything from negotiating player contracts to hassling over the lease at the Omni, the team's arena.

One of Ted's instructions to me was to promote heavily, to draw as many fans as possible, even though our team was designed to lose. Knowing nothing about basketball, I relied on my baseball knowledge to draw a big crowd to the opening game.

In baseball, when all else failed, fireworks always got us a big crowd. I knew I had to have fireworks to start the Hawks' season off right. But fireworks at a basketball game presented a new challenge. The games are played indoors. From a promoter's point of view, this was the perfect situation. No one had ever had a giant indoor fireworks show. If we could pull it off, it would be sensational. We decided to promote the opening game as "Basketball's Biggest Barn Burner Ever," claiming we would "blow the roof off the Omni."

Once we started promoting our basketball-fireworks spectacular, we had to find a way to do it. I checked with all my regular fireworks companies but none was willing to risk putting on an indoor show. Finally, I found K & K, a Japanese company that wanted my Braves business so badly it was willing to do anything. The Hawks show would test its capabilities.

With the fireworks show lined up and advertised, I set out to get approval from the Atlanta fire marshal. This may seem backwards. We probably should have gotten approval first, but that wasn't the way we operated. At the Braves, someone objected to virtually every promotion we had, but we had pulled so many oddball stunts by now that the police and fire departments had pretty much stopped complaining. Sometimes it took a few free tickets, but they always eventually came around.

In fact, we developed an aura of being beyond the bounds of

law and order. Once, for instance, I was given a speeding ticket for traveling ninety miles an hour on the freeway between Atlanta and Macon. When I got back to the office, I called the state patrol to see if I could mail in my fine rather than appear in court. The head of the state patrol responded by having the officer who had stopped me and taken my license deliver the license to my office that afternoon and apologize. I knew he had nothing to apologize for since I was guilty, but I wasn't going to argue about it.

So we assumed that getting an indoor fireworks show approved would be only a minor obstacle, but the fire marshal surprised us. He said our opening-night show was too dangerous and we couldn't hold it. I appealed to his civic pride, explaining that big crowds would be the only thing to save the Hawks. He didn't want it to be his fault when the team left the city, did he? That didn't work.

Finally, I just plain begged. The fire marshal made a deal with me. He asked us to ignite a sample of every rocket we intended to use in the show, one at a time, so he could make sure they would fall short of the Omni roof. We performed the test one afternoon inside the arena. Each rocket was lit, blasted off from the floor, and fell well short of the roof. Everything was okay. The show was approved.

The fire department laid down the rules. First, we had to cover the basketball floor immediately after the game with fire-proof material. Also, the fire department would listen to the game on the radio, and at the beginning of the fourth quarter their trucks would proceed to the Omni. Firemen with extinguishers would completely surround the court during the fireworks display. It sounded good to me.

We kept promoting the show, announcing that it would take place immediately after the Hawks opening-night game. Thousands of rockets, coordinated to music, would explode in the first indoor fireworks display in the history of the world (or at least the first we knew about).

I gave my instructions to Kay Kimura, who ran K & K Fireworks. "Nobody expects this show to be much," I told him, "so let's don't overdo it. Just don't let anyone get hurt."

But the Japanese have great pride, and Kay was committed to proving the excellence of his company. When the game ended, before a crowd of about eight thousand, which may not sound huge but was triple the crowd of the opening game a year earlier, the fireworks people went to work. A half-hour later, the most elaborate fireworks setup I had ever seen — and I'd seen a lot of them — was in place on the Omni floor. I suddenly realized I was in for a great show.

The lights of the Omni were turned off and the dramatic music from *2001: A Space Odyssey* started playing. Rockets, fired electronically, raced toward the Omni ceiling. The music changed to the *1812 Overture* and more rockets and special effects went off. Hundreds of rockets were flying all over the place. It was the most spectacular fireworks show I had ever seen. But I soon sensed I was in trouble.

First, I have never seen so much smoke in my life. When the lights came back on, it was minutes before I could see the people on the other side of the arena. Also, the rockets seemed like they were going higher than I remembered in the test. And finally, I didn't see any firemen.

The smoke went away eventually. But when it cleared, big black spots were visible all over the roof of the building. The rockets had literally blown the roof off the arena . . . or at least blown holes in it. It seems there's a law of physics which I knew nothing about but which had been dramatically demonstrated during the fireworks show. The fire marshal obviously didn't know this law either. The thrust of the rockets we had tested remained at a certain level when the rockets were fired individually, but a bunch of rockets packed closely and fired together produced considerably more thrust. It produced enough to bounce missiles off every inch of the Omni's roof.

For the next month, until the roof was fixed, the Omni leaked when it rained, making rainouts a real possibility for the Hawks. Also, the giant scoreboard that hung above the basketball court never worked right again.

Finally, there is also an answer to the mystery of the missing firemen. That particular day, Georgia Tech had a football game on the radio station that broadcasts the Hawks games too. The station decided to tape-delay the Hawks game so the football game could be broadcast live. That meant everything the Hawks' listeners heard had actually taken place an hour earlier; the basketball game the fire department was listening to had already happened. Just before the end of the broadcast, they got into their trucks and drove to the Omni, but by then the fireworks show had already ended and the crowd had gone home.

Regardless, we got the first basketball game of the season under our belts, and on top of that, the Hawks won the game. In fact, the players kept winning games. There was no explanation for it. Some people in the league said the team was so short, young, and inexperienced that it threw off the timing of the opposing teams in the league. Ten games into the year, the Hawks had the best record in the NBA—nine wins and only one loss.

The fans were happy. We were selling out almost every game. But Ted was furious. We were disobeying his orders. We weren't losing games. It was important to Ted's business that the team lose. He had told us that the FCC might soon rule that a television station in the top twenty TV markets would not be allowed to have its signal distributed to cable systems nationwide by satellite. Channel 17 in Atlanta might be shut out of the cable business. He would then have to shift his operations to his Charlotte station, which was not in the top twenty. The Hawks needed to be able to move to Charlotte. In fact, we were playing several of our home games in Charlotte during the season as a test.

Ted was also concerned that our winning would blow the number-one draft pick. He knew there was no way the team would be winning at the end of the season, but he was afraid it had already won enough to escape having the worst record in the league. I reminded Ted that I had told him earlier I knew nothing about basketball. I was doing everything I could to help us lose. I just didn't know enough about basketball to

figure out what to do. Regardless of excuses, we had dis-
obeyed Ted's orders.

Before too many more games, however, Ted also loved our
Cinderella team. As it charged up and down the court, he had
the organist play the theme from *Rocky*. The Hawks were
children in the land of giants, Davids who were regularly slay-
ing the Goliaths of the league.

Ted was right, however, that the Hawks weren't good
enough to keep winning. The outmanned team started to fal-
ter midway though the year, and attendance started to drop
off. As the chief promoter of the team, I was determined to set
records at the gate. Braves attendance was soaring each year. I
wanted the same thing with the Hawks. But it was much
tougher to do in the NBA. In baseball, attendance numbers
are carefully audited. The turnstile count is announced as
attendance each game, and only paid admissions are included
in the count. In basketball, there is no auditing process.
Teams just announced whatever attendance they wanted.
When the Hawks' season started, I was determined to use
honest attendance numbers—which was easy as long as the
crowds were big. However, as the season went along, our honest attendance wasn't staying far enough ahead of the phony
attendance numbers of the previous year.

Each night when the accurate attendance number was
given to me, I'd march over to Ted, who was sitting in his
chair next to the court, and whisper it in his ear. Early in the
year when the crowds were big, he'd smile and give me a
thumbs up. But as attendance started dropping off, Ted got
feisty. He wanted to know what the gate was the same date the
previous year, and this comparison of figures was getting
uncomfortable. So we did the only thing we could to stay out
of trouble and keep everyone happy. I'd huddle with the ticket
department each game and we'd make up the attendance
figure. We added just enough to the real crowd size to keep
Ted happy. It may not have been honest, but it saved us a lot of
grief. Also, it was proof that people can start believing things
they know aren't true. By the end of the season, we were

actually proud of the progress we had made in attendance. Our bogus figures were better than last year's.

Eventually I got into the swing of doing my jobs with both the Hawks and the Braves. I had never been the most organized person. So when I first started working in my baseball office each morning and my basketball office in the afternoon, it seemed someone was always showing up for a meeting at the wrong place. But after the initial confusion, I was going full speed, doing both jobs the same way and using pretty much the same mix of promotions for both baseball and basketball. In fact, the basketball arena was much more suited to promotions than the big, wide-open baseball stadium. It was cozy enough for the crowd to get a close look at everything, and the sound didn't echo like it did in the stadium.

As always, many of our promotions were giveaways to kids. We gave them basketballs, team shirts, team shorts, wristbands, gym bags, anything we thought might inspire them to come. We put a lot of emphasis on giveaway items that advertised the players or our team. We produced a life-size growth chart picturing seven-foot Tree Rollins. We gave away jigsaw puzzles depicting different players from the team. That may not sound so unusual now, but we were the only team doing it. It was a direct rip-off from baseball.

We even had our wet-T-shirt contest at a Hawks game, but this time the contestants had to stand in plastic swimming pools placed on the basketball floor. Somehow it wasn't the same.

We tried fireworks outside the Omni after a game, but nobody much cared. Bennie Koske, the Human Bomb, was one of my regulars at the Braves. He'd blow himself up at second base for $1,000, and I'd use him several times during a season. He'd climb into a wooden box, and the box would explode. Bennie would roll around on the ground for a couple of minutes and then climb to his feet to the cheers of the crowd. Once Bennie had the flu and made his wife get blown up in his place. She'd never done it before, and when she just lay flat on the ground after the explosion instead of rolling around, Bennie lost his temper and ran out there shouting for her to get up. He was afraid they'd forfeit the thousand bucks. Losing his temper was out of character for Bennie. Other than being a little hard of hearing, he was generally the perfect gentleman.

Inside the basketball arena, Bennie's explosion practically burst the eardrums of the fans, and the percussion finished off what was left of the scoreboard and blew out the giant doors—called elephant doors—at the end of the arena. Anyone walking by the doors outside the building when Bennie blew would have been in for a real jolt. Bennie was better for baseball.

We tried all kinds of entertainment in the building. We projected laser shows from the ceiling, using the basketball court as a screen. We even had concerts after the games featuring an assortment of second-tier stars like Jerry Lee Lewis. One thing that worked at the Hawks games that we couldn't do at the stadium was pranks. The basketball arena was so small that we could literally tell jokes and play tricks on the crowd.

One night prior to the game, an Arab sheik walked into the arena draped in full regalia and with an entourage trailing him. The entire group took their places in the courtside seating. The sportswriters and everyone else close enough to grab me were asking if I knew who it was. I told them I assumed the sheik was one of Ted's sailing friends.

At halftime, the sheik was introduced on the public-address system as the world's most famous Persian yachtsman, and the crowd was told he was going to make a special presentation at the game. The sheik walked up to a microphone on the court and told the crowd that he was a dear sailing friend of Ted Turner. He asked Ted to join him at the mike and then presented him with a "priceless" vase from King Tut's tomb. The King Tut exhibit, by the way, was very popular at the time and was on display in New Orleans. Ted told the sheik he was flattered but would rather see the vase given to one of the wonderful fans at the game that night. A barrel of tickets was hauled out on the court, and a lucky ticket was drawn for the vase.

Alas, the lucky ticket winner was the most inebriated fan at the game. The man stumbled down the aisle, fell over the gate that led to the court, and eventually staggered to the mike. He accepted the prized gift and thanked Ted and the sheik while waving it precariously in one hand. He finally dropped it, and it smashed into pieces. It was only a prank, but it had the fans gasping and groaning.

At the next game an old man in his eighties and a beautiful young blonde conspicuously made their way to the chair seats on the floor right next to the court. The old man walked feebly, using a cane, while the blonde pranced beside him in her mink coat. The crowd buzzed with comments about the couple.

During a timeout in the first half, she jumped up from her chair and took off her coat to reveal she was wearing nothing but a bikini. She then ran around the court with the old man furiously chasing after her. She finished her mad dash by jumping into Ted Turner's lap. Usually Ted was alerted to our promotions ahead of time. This time he had his wife, mother, and in-laws with him at the game, and we decided to catch him totally by surprise. We did. He enjoyed it, though, and the photo of Ted with the bikini-clad woman in his lap was on the front page of the paper the next day. Our motley basketball team was winning more games than anyone expected, and, as with the Braves, we were having a good time with our goofy promotions.

Just as I was getting used to working for the Hawks and Braves at the same time, Ted was letting the two teams run together in his mind. For a while, he wanted to make Hubie Brown the manager of the Braves in addition to his job as Hawks coach. Ted was impressed with what Hubie had been able to do with his team of cast-offs and rookies and decided he could probably do the same thing with the Braves. Eddie Johnson was a particularly quick rookie guard for the Hawks. Ted watched Johnson's quickness each game as a Hawk and decided he was much quicker than any Braves player. He started talking about doubling Eddie up as the Braves' short-stop. It took all of us to convince Ted to keep his players and coaches exclusive to one sport. We were lucky Bo Jackson hadn't come along yet.

We were having a good time getting the crowd in on the action at the Hawks games, and sometimes we went a little too far. One game we took a vocal vote during the game to select the World's Ugliest Man. Of all the candidates judged by cheers of the crowd, the referee of the game won in a land-side. He proceeded to rip the public-address mike from the scoring table. He didn't think our joke was so funny.

The team finally finished the year with a .500 record. Not only was Ted's fear of not getting the top draft pick realized; the Hawks even made the NBA playoffs.

Hubie had done an amazing job of coaching his rag-tag crew. It was the perfect team for his dictatorial brand of coaching. Hubie barked orders and the kids on the team responded. Veteran stars might not be so responsive to the way he would rant and rave from the start to the finish of each game. Occasionally a player got miffed. Tom McMillen once stopped in the middle of the court during a game and just stared at Hubie for what seemed like minutes.

Hubie was popular with the crowd. He was not only the most colorful coach in the league, but his volatility made him as interesting to watch as the game. Once, in a particularly close and nerve-wracking game, Hubie turned from the bench and pointed into the seats. "You," he yelled, looking midway up an aisle, "the redhead in the third seat on the eleventh row. You're the first 'ten' I've seen all year."

The Hawks were eliminated from championship contention early in the playoffs, but it had been a glorious year. Ted, just as he did in 1976 with the Braves, came to virtually every game and was jumping up and down and cheering at courtside. Ted never tried to get close to the Hawks players like he did the Braves, but it seemed obvious he enjoyed the game of basket-ball better than he did baseball.

By the end of the season, Ted adored Hubie and had forgotten all about his plans to lose, get the number-one draft pick, and move the team out of town. The Hawks' success was contributing to his status as a hero. But Hubie had not forgotten. At a reception in honor of Hubie's being named NBA Coach of the Year, Ted talked about how he knew Hubie would be able to build the Hawks into a winning team, how he had confidence in Hubie all along. When it came Hubie's time to speak, he commented on the early-season instructions to cut payroll and noted the lack of support from Ted. He ripped Ted apart in his acceptance speech, gave him no credit for the success of the team, and said it all happened despite Ted. As much as Ted had grown to like Hubie, Hubie did not return the affection.

After that, it was only a matter of time before Hubie was gone. He was Coach of the Year again the next season, but he never again had any support from Ted. In two years, he was fired.

As for me, I shifted back and forth from the Braves to the Hawks, filling both jobs for two years. The first year was fun and exciting, but the second became too much. I was doing too much and getting no satisfaction out of either job. When I was totally in baseball, I was an integral part of that fraternity, going to meetings, being chairman of several committees, and acting as emcee of various baseball events. I felt I belonged in baseball. Now I was part baseball, part basketball, and part personal promoter for Ted Turner. Also, eighty-one home baseball games and forty-one in basketball makes for a long, long year. It seemed I was with Ted Turner night and day, every day, and it was wearing me out.

19

THE PASSING

I was sitting at my desk in the trailer that had been my office for the past six years at spring training in West Palm Beach. The trailer even had a big sign with my name on it, and out in front of the stadium entrance was another sign with my name and an arrow pointing to the trailer. A parking space in the lot had "Hope" lettered on the post in front of it. I belonged here.

The phone rang, I picked it up, and it was Dee Woods. "Bob, Ted needs to talk to you," she said.

"Hope, what the hell are you doing down there in Florida?" he shouted over the phone. "You're supposed to be up here working on the Hawks."

I had decided to take a week and spend it with the baseball team in spring training. It wasn't the several-week stint I enjoyed every year, but I wanted quality time with the game I enjoyed. That game was not basketball.

I argued with Ted, and he allowed me to spend the week in Florida, but he obviously wasn't pleased. I was turning more and more of my work with the Braves over to my assistant, Randy Donaldson, and he was doing a good job. I didn't feel as needed as I once did.

We charged into the season with the same zeal as always. Attendance was growing, but Ted said he thought people were growing weary of all the crazy promotions. If a first ostrich race was a novelty, a second was more familiar, and a third was merely routine. The responsibility for creating excitement was leaving my hands and falling directly onto the team. People wanted to see big-league baseball played the way it was supposed to be played.

A month into the season, we were once again in last place, and the sportswriters and fans were losing their patience. Ted called a meeting on a Saturday afternoon in the stadium press lounge for him and Bill Lucas to talk to the media about the team. The media had been unusually rough. They had given us a break the past couple of years, even joined in on the fun. Now, they were voicing their disapproval loud and clear.

Bill Lucas tried to defend his youngsters in the lineup— Pat Rockett at shortstop and Junior Moore at third base. But the mood in the media and in the city had deteriorated completely. We were in our third straight last-place season, and there seemed to be no way out. The meeting broke up without resolution but with clear recognition that everybody was frustrated.

In June, pitcher Dick Ruthven was traded to the Phillies for relief pitcher Gene Garber. Ruthven stung the Braves' outfielders with his parting remark, "It's great to be away from those greyhounds in the Braves outfield." He was referring to rightfielder Gary Matthews and leftfielder Jeff Burroughs; both had decent bats but no speed.

We did, however, get some benefit out of Ruthven's swipe. We played off of his "greyhound" quote by holding Greyhound Day on the first Sunday he returned to Atlanta to pitch against the team. Randy Donaldson advised me to reconsider the promotion for fear it would motivate Ruthven to humiliate the Braves that day. I charged ahead with my plans. We had greyhound racing in the outfield before the game and played a country song titled "Thank God and Greyhound She's Gone" on the public-address system between innings. The promotion captured the imagination of the fans. We had a big crowd for Ruthven's return, and the crowd dutifully booed him for the nasty comments he had made about our "speedy" outfielders.

But Randy was right; Ruthven was inspired. He pitched the game of his life and shut out the Braves that day. To top that off, my phone at home started ringing with offers to buy the greyhounds I had for sale. Ruthven had placed a classified ad in the Atlanta newspapers with my phone number for people to call. I was losing my knack. Ted once told me that he and I were blessed with the "magic touch." It seemed my magic was slipping.

One day the phone rang and Dee warned me once again that Ted was about to get on the line, "Hope, tell me, what's wrong with the Braves?" he pleaded. Tired and frustrated, I told him the truth: "We just have a horseshit team." Actually, it was uncharacteristic of me to be so blunt, but those seemed to be the only words to sum up our baseball team. Ted was furious I would use such a description for his beloved players, but I was disgusted.

The season passed very slowly and without much fanfare. We drafted a third baseman out of college as our number-one pick. His name was Bob Horner and he insisted on playing for the Braves without having to go to the minor leagues first. We argued for a while that it was necessary to get minor-league seasoning, but he finally won out and became our starting third baseman. He did fine. In fact, he was Rookie of the Year in the league. It may be we weren't much different from playing in the minors that year.

When the season ended, I started to work on basketball again. The basketball team had survived their off-season intact without me, and after the surprising success of the previous season, pre-season ticket sales were way up. There wasn't much need there for my wacky promotions any more. But we did some anyway, if only for old times' sake. Stan Kasten was now well entrenched running the team, and it was getting better and better. The season would be an outstanding success.

Things may have been getting a little boring for all of us, including Ted. The SuperStation had now been up on the satellite and beamed out to cable systems for a couple of years. It was growing fast and needed little attention from the top. No one had any idea what to do about the Braves. It looked like they might lose forever. And to everyone's surprise, the Hawks were great and drawing big crowds with no trouble. All of us needed something exciting in our lives.

One night before a Hawks game, Ted led the discussion at the dinner table about what to do next. There really wasn't much need anymore for a broadcast signal to make the SuperStation work. Few people watched the transmitted signal of Channel 17 anyway. Ted suggested that maybe it was time to pull the plug on the broadcast signal and become the first major cable-only network. The TV sales staff objected to that idea. It was too radical. It would scare off advertisers.

Someone suggested we start a sports-only cable channel. It would be possible for us to take the Braves and Hawks games and use them as the base programming for an all-sports channel. But that presented the problem of having to replace the Braves and Hawks on the SuperStation, where they were both important programming. That wouldn't work.

Someone mentioned the idea of an all-music TV network, playing hit songs just like a radio station. Nobody thought that was a good idea. Nothing seemed more boring than watching pictures while listening to music. It wouldn't work.

Then someone mentioned an all-news cable network. Ted said he had thought about the idea but was afraid no one would tune in very long. We compared it to all-news radio, where people tuned in and then tuned out quickly after they heard the news. Maybe people didn't have to sit and watch for hours. Maybe a news channel was the best idea.

Turner said what we'd all heard him say before: "I hate the news. News is evil. It makes people feel bad. I don't want anything to do with news." After all, Channel 17 showed news only because the FCC required it, and we got even by showing it at three in the morning.

Someone said maybe it could be done like the "Today Show," more like a twenty-four-hour talk show with news interspersed. That sounded better than expecting people to sit and just watch the news hour after hour.

Ted jumped up. "If we do the news on cable only and don't have a broadcast signal, the FCC can't tell us what we can and can't show, right?" he shouted. "Right," we conceded.

"Then we can show the most gory murder, like when a man kills his wife or girlfriend and chops her up in little bitty pieces and puts her in the freezer, right?" he said gleefully. "Right," we agreed, shaking our heads.

That was the end of the dinner, and we all left to go to the game. Over the next few weeks, Ted started working to put together his cable network that would be "like a twenty-four-hour 'Today Show'" and would show people "chopped up in little bitty pieces." Ted got more serious about the news over the next few months. The new project became CNN.

As the 1979 baseball season started, there wasn't much reason for any of us to feel the team was improving. We added no free agents and made no trades in the off-season. Bill Lucas and Ted Turner were having a difficult time with Bob Horner's agent, a gruff, squatty Texan named Bucky Woy. Bill seemed particularly perplexed by the situation, and it was obvious Ted simply didn't like Woy, which didn't make life any easier for Bill. Ted had had run-ins with agents in the past. Once he got into the name-calling contest with agent Jerry Kapstein. When a Jewish organization accused Ted of making anti-Semitic remarks about Kapstein, Ted extended a written apology. He signed it, "Yours in Christ."

Dealing with Ted and Bucky Woy was a challenge for Bill. One afternoon I heard Ted and Bill having a verbal brawl in Ted's office over what to do. My phone rang at three-thirty the next morning. It was a reporter from the *Atlanta Constitution* asking about the condition of Bill Lucas.

Bill, the forty-five-year-old general manager of the Braves, had been rushed to the hospital. The reporter wanted more information. It was the first I had heard about it, but I had the strange feeling that overwhelms you when you instinctively know something terrible has happened.

I called Braves business manager Charles Sanders, asking if he had heard anything. He hadn't. So I drove to pick up Charles, and the two of us went to South Fulton Hospital in south Atlanta. In the lobby, Hank Aaron and Bill's teenage children were waiting. Bill had suffered an apparent stroke and was unconscious. They were waiting to hear from the doctors.

I was thirty-two years old and still felt baseball was meant to be fun. Losing seemed miserable on one scale, but this was real misery. I went to a waiting room to see Bill's wife, Rubye. She was in there by herself and asked me to stay. She told me how Bill had clutched his head and fallen over. When he wouldn't respond, they called an ambulance. Now, suddenly, she was waiting to find out what had happened, suspecting the worst.

Bill was entering his third season as the only black general manager in major-league baseball. He had built the Braves' farm system before becoming head of the big-league team and had staunchly defended the young players who he felt would someday lead the big-league Braves to a pennant. Bill felt the pressures of losing more than anyone else. It seemed absurd to think a losing baseball team could lead to this. But it also seemed like a real possibility.

Rubye, whom I'd known since I first joined the team as a college freshman, was generally a very reserved woman. She was a schoolteacher and always the picture of dignity. But this morning she was sobbing uncontrollably. We waited for a couple of hours without hearing anything. At one point a bed with Bill on it was rolled past the open door, and Rubye lunged to the floor weeping. Mostly, she sat next to me, holding on to my arm. In a way I was pleased to be there by her side. At the same time, I had never been through anything like this and felt awkward and incompetent. Charles sat in a chair across the room, puffing on his pipe. I realized that people are capable of responding in different ways, and I was the only one at the hospital at the time who could attempt to comfort Rubye.

We were all numb the next few hours. A doctor finally came

in and told us Bill was still unconscious. He had shown no signs of snapping out of a coma, and they were about to give him a brain scan. A couple of hours later, the doctor said there were no signs of brain-wave activity, but they would keep him on life support systems and continue to check. The situation looked bleak.

As morning came, others started showing up. Paul Snyder, who had been Bill's assistant for years and now worked with Hank to head the minor-league system, came by. Dick Cecil came and took control of the hospital arrangements. I remained by Rubye's side. Ted arrived and told Rubye not to worry, that whatever happened, the kids' college would be taken care of. Then, later in the day, we drove her home to rest.

Several of us returned to the hospital. We stood next to Bill's body as he breathed with the aid of machines, and we all tried to talk to him, encourage him, hoping he would hear and respond. As I drove out of the hospital parking lot behind Ted's car, the parking attendant told me with pride that he had just met Ted Turner in the car ahead. "Can you believe he drives a Toyota?" he asked. Later in the day, the doctor finally told Rubye there was no hope. Bill was brain-dead, and the systems were turned off.

Bill was vibrant and youthful. His death was a total shock. I had never been so close to someone's death. At the hospital, waiting with Rubye was the toughest thing I had ever done. The ostrich race, Ted's pushing a baseball with his nose, the wet-T-shirt contest, and every other promotion we had run in the past seemed so distant and strange when we talked about promoting this particular season. When I first joined the Braves in college, I felt I had the greatest job in the world. I went to bed each night excited about getting up the next morning. Things seemed to be changing so quickly.

The days between Bill's death and his funeral were wrenching. When the press called and wanted comments from the team, all answers were out of kilter with the baseball I had known. There could be no cute or flip comments. It was not a game. Last place became trivial even to the most cynical sportswriter. When I was asked to appear on a Braves pre-game television show to talk about Bill, my mind went blank. I could think of nothing to say, a real contrast to the typical interview with me when it was tough to shut me up.

Dick Cecil handled most of the funeral details. I'm the one who always wanted to make everything into a circus, but even I felt the funeral was getting way out of hand. I assume there is no way of stopping people from coming from all over the country, but there were hundreds of people on hand.

Ted gave a eulogy. He talked about Bill's being in the "big baseball league in the sky" and said he was now general manager of a team with "Babe Ruth, Ty Cobb, Lou Gerhig" and all the great Hall of Famers. It seemed so inappropriate, but as always, because it was Ted, people acted like it was brilliant.

Al Thornwell and Mike Gearon both called me the next couple of days to tip me off that Ted was likely to ask me to replace Bill as the team's general manager. Both said Ted asked them if they thought I knew enough about player talent to do the job. Both told Ted I did. Mike finally called me at home to say Ted had made up his mind and I would be his choice. He said Ted had gotten some pressure to go outside the organization to pick a top baseball official from another team, someone who had built a winning team. But Ted felt I had always gotten the job done for him, and he wanted to give me the chance. Ted would call me the next morning.

"Act surprised," Mike instructed.

I had a strange feeling of excitement and depression at the same time. At thirty-two, I'd be the youngest general manager in the game. I was certain I'd do a great job, and it was the job that I had set as my goal. But the circumstances made all considerations seem different. Still, I was proud to be asked and intent on doing a great job. I'd make the Braves a winner.

The next morning Ted called and said he needed to see me in his office that afternoon. I was ready. Just in case he'd want to see it, I wrote a plan on how I would staff the front office, listing the changes I would make and the reasons why. Since I hadn't come up through the scouting or player-development area and knew less about player issues than anything else, I identified the person I would bring in to be my assistant on the player-personnel side of the business. Ted would be pleased.

When I arrived at his office, Ted was solemn. He simply asked me to sit down. "Hope, I'm turning the team over to you," he said. "I've thought about it for a long time." As Ted talked, he showed the strain of the past few days.

"You've done a good job, and you're the only one with the team who could replace Bill," he continued. "I've had a lot of pressure to hire someone from the outside. I don't want to put too much pressure on you. I don't want you to die, too. I'm going to name you the interim general mananger. Then, after you've been in the job for a while and people are used to you, we'll make it permanent. If it doesn't work out, you can go back to doing what you do now."

I sat there and listened. Then I assured him I could do the job. I started to tell him some of the things I wanted to do to reorganize the office staff, but he didn't want to listen.

"The only thing that bothers me about you is you have a mind of your own," Ted remarked. "When I tell you what I want you to do, you listen but then do whatever you were going to do in the first place. I've let you do that because you've done a good job, but I know when I turn the team over to you, I will lose control. I'm willing to do that. I'll stay out of the way."

I took a few minutes to tell Ted about a person I'd identified to bring in as my assistant, the one to be my player-personnel expert. His name was John Schuerholz. He was the farm director of the Kansas City Royals. I didn't tell Ted I met John when he zeroed in on our Farrah Fawcett look-alike winner at the All-Star Game, but that wasn't necessary. "He's the brightest young guy I've met in the game," I said.

It was Friday, and Ted said to get back with him Monday to work out the details of my new job. Even as we talked, I could tell Ted still had some doubts.

I called Susan to tell her the news. "I'm going to be the new general manager of the Braves." I also called my mom and dad. I wanted to tell someone else, but knew I couldn't risk the news getting back to Ted, which would sour the whole deal.

As I was leaving the stadium that day with Wayne Minshew, who now worked in the Braves' publicity department, a young television reporter from Atlanta's Channel 5 stopped us. She wanted an interview about Bill's death and what the Braves would do for a replacement. We had never met her before. She was fresh out of the University of Georgia, and her name was Deborah Norville. I told her I'd be happy to talk. She said she'd rather interview Wayne, that I looked too young. That made me more determined than ever that I wanted the job. I wanted to tell her, "Look, don't you know who I am? I'm the new general manager."

By Monday, I was anxious to meet with Ted. I waited for his call. When it didn't come, I placed a call to him, only to be told he wasn't available and would get back to me later. I still hadn't heard from him Tuesday, despite a couple of other attempts to reach him. The press called me to ask about a rumor that John Mullen of the Houston Astros was being hired to replace Bill Lucas.

Tuesday night we had a game at the stadium, and Ted was sitting in his usual spot down by the Braves' dugout. I had a personal policy never to go sit by him during a game. There were two types of people in the organization — those who pandered to him and sat next to him all the time and those who worked hard and responded when called on. I resolutely placed myself in the second category. That night I had no choice. I went down to his box seats and plopped down right next to him.

"Well, Ted, am I or not?" I asked with a false air of comfort.

Ted normally looked right in my eyes when he talked to me. This time he stammered and hesitated. I knew the answer before he opened his mouth.

"Hope, I thought about it more this weekend," he said. "You're just too valuable to me to isolate on just baseball. I need you too many places."

I knew that was bull. I got up and walked away without saying a word. I didn't want to hear any more.

The next day, Ted called to say he had talked to more people and felt he needed to get a top-flight "baseball man" from another team. After all, I was basically a public relations man. He said the team's manager, Bobby Cox, was upset by the idea of my taking over. Also, he had asked around about John Schuerholz and was told he was a bad choice. (Coincidentally, Schuerholz is now the new general manager of the Braves, although I had nothing to do with his selection.)

Whatever the reason, I knew it was too late to change Ted's mind back in my favor. And after thinking about it, I wasn't sure being a big-league general manager was all I had thought it would be. Your success is based on a group of players, and if they can't play or won't play, you fail. You can't hit for them; you can't pitch for them. John Mullen of the Astros was hired.

I went about the task of doing my old job . . . or make that jobs. I was running the marketing operations of the Braves and the Hawks and still handling most of Ted's personal publicity and promotion. As he would tell people, "We have no public relations department at Turner Broadcasting. Just Hope."

All the zany promotions that had made me feel like such a star in the past now made me feel uncomfortably flaky. Susan used to kid me by saying, "It may be fun to be the village idiot, but it's not so much fun being married to him." I wasn't sure I wanted to be the village idiot any more.

The Coca-Cola Company had contacted me several times about coming to work for them. This time I accepted. Now all I had to do was tell Ted.

I let the rumor mill work in my favor. I told everyone around Ted, hoping he'd hear and wouldn't be shocked when I went in to tell him. "Shock" may not be the right word. I really didn't expect to hurt his feelings, and I really didn't think I was as important to Ted as I had been in the past. After all, my job was to make him famous. Now he was. I had learned over the years, however, that it is best not to catch Ted by surprise.

When I finally went to his office, I could tell he already knew. He tried to be nice and stay calm, but he was noticeably upset. I felt like a child announcing I was leaving home. Ted tried to wish me well, but in the end he just couldn't bring himself to do it.

"Coca-Cola's a stale old company, with stale old products and stale old people," he told me as I walked out the door.

20

LIFE AFTER BASEBALL

Growing up in Atlanta, you can't help being intrigued by the lore of the great enterprise that took a dark, sweet, bubbly liquid and built it into a world institution. Robert Woodruff, the man who transformed Coca-Cola into a symbol of world friendship, is every bit as much a legend in Atlanta as Babe Ruth is in baseball. Coke is special, and so is the company that makes it. However, the Coca-Cola Company is huge — not like my little Braves. I jumped right into my new job, thinking I would be involved in everything the company did, just like at the Braves. I'd hang around the president, we'd decide to do great things, and then we'd go do them. The reality was I only saw the president a half-dozen times in two years.

One of them occurred on an elevator the morning after his secretary had asked me to get him tickets to a Hawks game. I got Ted's tickets right down on the court. I watched during the game as the president of Coca-Cola became so emotionally wrapped up in the game that he charged out onto the court when the referee made a "bad" call against the home-team Hawks. I mentioned on the elevator that it was pretty embarrassing for an employee to see the president of the company fighting with a referee. I chuckled and got off when the elevator stopped at my floor. That afternoon I spent most of my time in offices of top executives being lectured on not embarrassing the president in public. "Embarrass him?" I thought. "I got him tickets and he embarrassed me." Coke was great, but it wasn't like life with Ted.

I charged into my job of inventing promotions for Coke with the same vigor I had while at the Braves. I was initially given the assignment to come up with a promotion for Mr. PiBB, the toughest sell of all the soft drinks. Nobody had ever been able to develop a successful promotion for Mr. PiBB, which happens to taste exactly like Dr. Pepper. However, when you work at Coke, you can't say it tastes like anything that anyone else makes. When Mr. PiBB was first introduced, the president was asked if it was supposed to taste like Dr. Pepper. "I don't know," he cleverly replied. "I've never tasted Dr. Pepper."

My promotion for Mr. PiBB was a smash hit. It was called the PiBB Girl Contest. I hired the artist who painted the famous Breck Shampoo portraits to concoct a fictitious lady we called the PiBB Girl. She had the facial features of different celebrities — the eyes of Susan Anton, the nose of Debbie Boone, the mouth of Brooke Shields, the hair of another star, and so on. It was a great idea. We launched a search to find the person who looked most like the PiBB Girl. The winner would get $5,000. The response to the promotion was terrific. We got thousands of entries almost immediately. Local beauty contests were being held all over the country. The bottlers, the key people who sell the soft drinks in local communities, loved the promotion. Publicity about the program appeared on "Good Morning America" and in newspapers across the nation.

When I was at the Braves, I once overheard Ted's secretary, Phyllis Collins, tell someone that I was such an amazing promotional talent, there were no bounds to what I might be able to accomplish if I worked for a big company. The PiBB Girl Contest, in my opinion, was the first evidence that Phyllis was right.

But then a small glitch appeared. The company received a letter from the headmaster of a school in Chicago complaining that the PiBB Girl was white. Thus, he concluded, the promotion was racist. All hell broke loose. Over the next few days, I met every top officer of the Coca-Cola Company, and none was in a very good mood. They all asked how I could be so stupid as to have done such a thing. I had no answer.

However, the top ranks of the Coca-Cola Company are filled with bright people who have done many not-so-bright things in their lives. So each meeting included an off-the-record account of a big blunder one of them had made during his or her career. Then I was dismissed, chastised but also assured that I was not to let one promotional stumble dampen my enthusiasm. That didn't make the PiBB Girl problems go away. The company sent word to all the bottlers to halt the promotion immediately, winners were quietly selected, and an attorney was sent around the country to meet with each winner and secretly award her a prize.

I was sent to California for a couple of weeks to work in grocery stores, a move designed to get me out of the line of fire until the shooting stopped. The PiBB Girl was the Easter-Egg Hunt revisited. Only this time I didn't slide right by.

It soon became evident that Coca-Cola did not want or, for that matter, need ostrich races, home-plate weddings, or even a single wet-T-shirt contest. My plan to dazzle everyone, race right to the top of the company, and hang around the president was stalled. In fact, I didn't even know the president, and when I finally met him, they sent me to California for my own good.

I did have modest success at Coke whenever called on to help on programs related to baseball. Once, for instance, we got word that dreaded Pepsi had just signed a contract to become the exclusive soft-drink sponsor of Major League Baseball. I got a wonderful memo from Roberto Goizueta, Coke's chairman of the board, noting that "it pains my heart to see Pepsi disrupt the long-treasured association that Coke has had with the game of baseball." I agreed with him heartily. It became my assignment to sabotage Pepsi's new baseball deal.

The "knock Pepsi out of baseball" program was right up

my alley; I was back in my briar patch. Pepsi had spent $16 million to become the sponsor of baseball; I asked for just $30,000 to kick them out. I found out that John Sculley, the president of Pepsi-Cola, was scheduled to make the announcement of the new Pepsi-baseball agreement at the winter meetings, which would take place in Toronto. The announcement would be featured at a banquet in the middle of the week.

I went to work. First, I called the organizers of the winter meetings and offered free entertainment for the banquet. The Toronto Blue Jays were making the arrangements for the meetings, and Blue Jays president Peter Bavasi, a good friend of mine, was happy to cooperate. I arranged for the entertainment at the banquet where Mr. Sculley was to make his announcement to be the Coca-Cola Spotlight Orchestra, accompanied by the Coca-Cola Spotlight Singers. They would perform an array of popular hits, including music from Coke commercials. For the entire evening the audience, and Mr. Sculley, would be serenaded with music like "Have a Coke and a Smile" and "I'd Like to Teach the World to Sing," mixed in with contemporary hits. By the way, there was no Coca-Cola Spotlight Orchestra until this moment. We invented it for the affair.

I also had "Coca-Cola Welcomes Baseball" posters printed and put them all over the hotel and in every store window and restaurant within walking distance of the meetings. Everyone who attended the meetings arrived to see a robot shaped like a can of Coca-Cola performing in the hotel lobby. They received a "Two Great American Pastimes: Coca-Cola and Baseball" poster as a gift and were invited to the Coca-Cola hospitality suite. Pepsi had a hospitality suite, too, so I bribed the Pepsi hostesses to wear Coca-Cola buttons, shirts, and caps. The result was exactly what we hoped. John Sculley showed up at the meetings, turned around, and went home. The announcement was never made.

I had taken a step toward recovery from the PiBB Girl fiasco.

At the end of my first year at the Coca-Cola Company, I was surprised when my bosses reviewed my work and gave me a "superior" rating on my performance appraisal. They told me I was two years away from being ready to be marketing director of the company and even had the potential to run it some day. "Boy, are they in trouble," I thought.

My second year at Coke was more of the same—walking the fine line between doing a good job and getting in trouble. I was put in charge of Coke's involvement in the 1984 Olympic Games in Los Angeles and worked feverishly to put together a thorough plan to take maximum advantage of the opportunity. I presented my plan over and over to management groups, refining and polishing it each time. They loved it. Finally it was time to present it to the president for approval. I had it all on slides and video, and I presented with perfection the same Olympic plan that virtually every Coke executive up to the presidential level had loved. He hated it. Now I had to start all over again.

It was completely different from working with Ted, where a great idea was a great idea, even if it was scribbled on a sheet of paper. With Ted, we'd talk and then we'd do. In this big company, I had gone through months of planning and preparation, only to get shot down in the last meeting and have to start again from scratch. By mid-year, I was tired of the corporate bureaucracy. I wasn't used to dealing with it and didn't deal with it well. I felt I was spending most of my time sending memos and preparing presentations for things that never happened. I wanted to do something and see results.

Former Braves pitcher Pat Jarvis and I had gone to the Masters Golf Tournament and were having dinner afterwards when we had an idea. For all the records Hank Aaron set in Atlanta, there was no tribute to him in the city. St. Louis, for example, had a statue of Stan Musial, so we decided to raise the money to build one of Hank in Atlanta. Over the next few months, my spare time was devoted to raising the $100,000 necessary to have a bronze figure of Hank hitting homer 715 placed outside the stadium where everyone attending a game could see it. I was thrilled to do it and even more thrilled by Hank's reaction. He told me he sometimes gets in his car when he's depressed and drives by the statue, just looking out the window at it. It lifts his spirits. That lifted mine.

At the end of my second year at Coke, I was once again told I was doing a good job and that I'd be put on the "fast track." I wasn't sure exactly what that meant but was sure it had to be good. Well, the first thing it meant was that I had to start acting like "senior management." The plan was to send me to a place called the Aspen School for training—kind of a charm school for senior executives. That would give me the polish I needed. From now on, I could wear only blue, gray, or black suits and only white long-sleeved shirts. I could wear no brown or green. All my ties had to be conservative, with conventional stripes or a subtle print. Also, I had to stop talking to people in the halls and elevators. At first I thought this was a joke, but I soon realized it was deadly serious. I know I was supposed to be excited, but I was more depressed. Granted, I may have been guilty of wearing brown loafers sometimes, or a sports coat and slacks rather than a suit, but I felt insulted. Besides, I dressed better than Ted Turner, and he was rich and famous.

Over the next few weeks I decided the Coca-Cola Company just wasn't for me. I was more certain than ever that it was a marvelous company, but my style of promotion—in fact, my style in general—didn't seem to fit the mold. I was having problems everywhere I turned. The first year my boss was Bruce Gilbert, who had been the vice president of marketing during Coke's most glorious marketing years. Bruce was in his fifties and seemed every bit as bright and innovative as Ted. Then I was transferred to work for someone else who made me take a handwriting test and gave me a written exam on how to treat a boss. The exam had questions like "When confronted with a difficult issue, do you tell the boss what you think he wants to hear or the truth?" I figured the boss would want to know the truth. On this test that was the wrong answer. The object was to always make the boss look and feel good . . . regardless. I never found out how I did on the handwriting test, and I was afraid to ask.

I did get to do a few things at Coke that were my style. When we needed a big event to promote Tab in San Francisco, I shot off fireworks from Alcatraz. When Houston wanted to fend off aggressive Pepsi growth, I put on a "Real Things of Houston" parade that drew 200,000 people to an event that consisted entirely of Coca-Cola floats.

While I was contemplating what to do, a gregarious and controversial Atlanta public relations man took me to lunch and asked me to join his firm. Bob Cohn was chairman of Cohn & Wolfe, a small agency that had just completed a successful Winter Olympics assignment for Coke. Bob proposed a deal to me. His firm was tiny, not big enough to build much of a retirement fund for him. He asked me to work for him for ten years, then pay him for ten years. The firm would then be mine. In essence, ten percent of his stock would accrue to me each year until I had it all. Then I'd pay him off over the next ten years. That would be his retirement plan. It sounded like a strange deal, but I liked Bob Cohn and was ready for something new. I took it.

Bob and I turned out to be a great combination. In the first year we tripled the size of the firm. Cohn & Wolfe became the fastest-growing public relations firm in the world. More important, even though I was still in the "serious" business world, I was having fun again. The firm was big enough to have great challenges, yet small enough to enjoy the chase and feel the excitement of each success or failure. We worked on major projects for Coca-Cola, like the introductions of Diet Coke and New Coke, and our client list included several other impressive names—Marriott, Ford Motor Company, Federal Express, and Philip Morris, to name a few. Occasionally, my Braves experience would come in handy.

When Coke changed its formula and introduced New Coke, they needed a huge public event put together in four days. Cohn & Wolfe assembled a massive circus in a public park in the middle of downtown Atlanta, and we called our event

"Step Right Up for the Greatest New Taste on Earth." I used my contacts from Braves days to locate two traveling circus troupes and instantly rerouted them to Atlanta. We draped all the buildings surrounding the park with Coca-Cola banners, shot fireworks from the tops of the buildings, and had singers and dancers performing all day on a stage next to the outdoor three-ring spectacular. I was proud. I knew this was something virtually no one but I could pull off so smoothly or quickly. At the event's noon highlight, the "new taste" was introduced to the city with a "who's who" gathering of Atlanta celebrities on hand. When Roberto Goizueta asked me when the celebrity group was scheduled to go on, I turned to an assistant for the answer: "They're on right after the elephants and the human cannon." It was just like the old days.

As the circus apparatus was being taken down that night, a vaguely familiar man walked up to me and asked, "Aren't you Bob Hope?" I nodded. "I'm Bennie the Bomb," he said. "I just want to tell you how much we circus people miss you in baseball. You were good for fifteen or twenty blasts a year."

Occasionally even Ted would call for help. When only a few tickets had been sold just ten days before a Hawks opening night, Stan Kasten offered $2,000 for an idea to shake them out of the doldrums. I told him to give me a day to think about it. When he called back the next morning, I told him I had the solution: "Mohawks for the Hawks." Every fan at the game willing to get a Mohawk haircut at halftime would get in the game free. In no time every disc jockey in town was talking up the promotion, and the tickets started moving. Only fifteen fans actually got their Mohawks, but the Omni was full. The old "village idiot" theory had succeeded once again.

Soon giant New York-based Burson-Marsteller bought Cohn & Wolfe, and after a couple of years CEO Jim Dowling asked me to move to New York. I was excited about the move but was sure my chances of dabbling in baseball would be gone forever. Burson-Marsteller had more than sixty offices around the world and thousands of employees. It had more people in its New York office than every Atlanta firm combined. And most of its work seemed to be for highly important clients. For instance, when a chemical company's employees were surrounded by a rebel army in a third-world country, the company called Burson-Marsteller. Like magic, the employees were released within twenty minutes. When Tylenol was sabotaged, Burson-Marsteller was called in. This was a very big, very serious company. Nevertheless, the need for my "specialty" still surfaced occasionally.

I was invited to speak to a business group in Miami, and a month beforehand they asked if I could talk about the upcoming expansion of the National League. Tampa and Orlando were among the dozen cities trying to get one of the two expansion franchises, and although Miami was not yet in the chase, a couple of groups were talking about entering. The audience wanted to know what Miami's chances of getting a team might be. I knew a lot about recent expansions in the other sports leagues. I had initiated Charlotte's successful effort to get a National Basketball Association team by setting up a meeting with David Stern, the commissioner. I had also planned a successful campaign for Ottawa to win a National Hockey League franchise. In fact, I was elected to the board of directors of the Ottawa Senators of the NHL. I knew little about the current baseball situation but was eager to catch up, and the speech prompted me to learn.

I showed up in Miami with a lot of information. I told the group that the race to get the two new teams would be hotly contested but there was no clear leader at the time. Even though other cities had been trying to get franchises for years, untimely events like the death of the commissioner and a spring-training lockout had put all contenders back on the starting line. I concluded by saying that if Miami decided it wanted a team, it could probably get one . . . at least, in my opinion. After the speech a stranger approached, gave me his business card, and asked me to give him a call. His name was Don Smiley and he worked for BLOCKBUSTER Entertainment Corporation.

I called Mr. Smiley, and he explained to me that BLOCK-

BUSTER Entertainment was the company that operated nearly two thousand BLOCKBUSTER video stores, and the chairman of the company, H. Wayne Huizenga, wanted me to visit him the next week. I went to the firm's headquarters in Fort Lauderdale and spent a day with Mr. Huizenga and Mr. Smiley. Mr. Huizenga said he had read a copy of my speech and was impressed. He told me he was thinking about going after an expansion team for the area and wanted to know if I honestly thought a campaign could be successful. I told him I did.

I soon learned that Mr. Huizenga was one of the most successful businessmen in the world. Before building BLOCK-BUSTER into the largest of all video rental and retail chains, he was founder of Waste Management, Inc., the largest solid-waste disposal company in the world. No one else in the history of business had ever built two such successful companies in two different industries.

A few weeks after our meeting, Mr. Huizenga visited me in New York to tell me he was buying half of Joe Robbie Stadium, where the Dolphins of the NFL play, and would renovate it so that big-league baseball could be played there. He was ready for me and Burson-Marsteller to help him get his team. The chase was on once again.

21

WATCHING FROM
THE OUTSIDE

I was sitting in the first-class section of a flight out of Toronto reading a newspaper as the other passengers got on the plane when I heard, "Oh no, Hope, they've done it to you too."

It was Ted Turner walking through the first-class section on the way back to his seat in coach, and he was commenting that I was now acting like the "muckety-mucks" he had always hated with such intensity. I was sitting in first class.

Once the plane took off and was in the air, Ted came back up to first class and asked the flight attendant if he could sit with me. The flight attendant said not unless he had a first class ticket, so he asked if I could go back to coach and sit with him. She said that would have to be my decision. Ted urged me to come back and sit with him, and I agreed. He grabbed my ticket out of my hand and gave it to the man next to him. "Here, go sit in first class," he ordered the stranger.

As soon as I sat down, Ted shouted to the people around him, "This is my pal, Hope. He had a first-class ticket but gave it up to come sit with me. Somebody buy him a drink."

Ted and I sat there and talked about the Braves. He talked with fondness about his ostrich race, but remembered that he didn't win. Then he recalled with pride having won the bathtub race. He talked about the frustrations of losing and the hope for winning in the future.

"When we finally get in the World Series, we're going to sit with each other, okay?" he asked. I smiled and said, "Okay." "Pals forever?" he asked, reaching out his hand to shake. "Pals forever," I responded, reaching out my hand. It gave new meaning to what seemed like a flip sign-off at the bottom of his letters to me, "Your pal, Ted Turner."

Some time later I was attending my first senior managers meeting of Burson-Marsteller. About three hundred representatives of the firm's worldwide system of offices were meeting in a New York ballroom. I was proud to be there. After years of trying, I felt I had finally overcome the wild-man image of my baseball past and had arrived on the scene as a "real" businessman. I was a counselor for a big, important firm, and no one in that room would know it had ever been any different.

A guest speaker at the meeting was former baseball commissioner Bowie Kuhn.

"We have someone with us," the moderator began, "who I'd like to recognize at this time. Last night I bought a book entitled *The Baseball Hall of Shame*. I will read you an excerpt from the book." I had never heard of the book and thought he was introducing Commissioner Kuhn.

The moderator started reading: "Baseball promotions are a means of scoring big at the gate even if the home team is losing big on the field. Management sometimes has felt that the fans want more than runs, hits, and errors; that the game itself can't make it without some gimmick or giveaways. But some promotions have the taste and sophistication of a TV game show gone mad."

At that point I knew I was in trouble; my heart started to sink.

"For 'The Most Undignified Ballpark Promotions,' The Baseball Hall of Shame inducts the following: Atlanta Braves Promotions, 1972-1979."

I listened apprehensively as he continued to read.

"During the 1970s, the Atlanta Braves spent most of their time down at the bottom of the barrel looking up at the rest of the division. And while they were down there, they scraped together some of the most absurd promotions ever concocted. The guy who came up with the ludicrous stunts was the Braves' publicity director, Bob Hope."

I couldn't believe it. Everyone in the room was about to find out my secret.

"'Shame is the only word to describe what we did,' said Hope. 'The Braves finished in last place four straight years. So as long as the team was losing games, we in the promotion department had nothing to lose.'

"Hope arranged for otherwise sane, normal people to race around on camels and ostriches and throw cow chips at each other. For 'Headlock and Wedlock Night,' thirty-four couples were married at homeplate in a mass wedding which was followed by professional wrestlers demonstrating their own peculiar embraces.

"One bizarre promotion nearly caused a fatality. An Atlanta disc jockey dove head-first into the world's largest ice cream sundae. Nobody told him that ice cream has a consistency like quicksand. The poor guy slowly sank out of sight in the goo. He was almost gone when guards pulled him out and revived him.

"Then there was the Wet-T-shirt Contest . . . ."

At this point, as I was trying my best to disappear, the speaker singled me out and asked me to stand. I guess I did, though I've tried to suppress the memory.

I can't shake my Braves past. It's part of me. I'm part of it. Once my cover was blown at the Burson-Marsteller meeting in New York, I was asked if I would invite Ted Turner to talk to the employees of the New York office. Ted stood up to address the group, and the first words out of his mouth were, "I was happy to be invited here by Bob Hope. Bob and I both are proof that you do things in your twenties that you don't do in your forties."

That's true. But maybe the Braves will do something in my forties that they didn't do in my twenties.

Win!

INDEX